TAKE SIX
MORE
COOKS

for Sara Jane

Christmas '90

Love and happy cooking

Julia & Michael.

Lobster Served Slightly Warm with Two Sauces **Gunn Eriksen** PAGE 42

Take Six More Cooks

Kay Avila

THAMES MACDONALD

A THAMES MACDONALD BOOK

First published in Great Britain in 1988
by Macdonald & Co (Publishers) Ltd
London & Sydney

A member of BPCC plc

British Library Cataloguing in Publication Data
Take six more cooks.
    1. Cookery, International
    1. Avila, Kay
    641.5   TX725.A1

    ISBN 0–356–15402–5

Filmset by August Filmsetting, Haydock, St Helens

Printed and bound in Great Britain by Purnell Book
Production, a member of BPCC plc

Editor: Catherine Rubinstein
Designer: Ingrid Mason
Photographer: Grant Symon
Stylist: Dee Martyn
Home Economist: Jane Suthering
Illustrator: Susan Alcantarilla
Art Director: Linda Cole
Indexer: Martin Noble

Macdonald & Co (Publishers) Ltd
Greater London House
Hampstead Road
London NW1 7QX

Contents

Introduction

It is four and a half years since the first series of *Take Six Cooks* was made, and it is quite extraordinary how changed our consciousness is about food. Chefs now enjoy a status unthinkable five years ago. At last, cooking has been accepted into the ranks of the professions, as of course it should have been years ago. Any self-consciousness – and there has been quite a lot, especially when nouvelle cuisine was 'cult' – has thankfully almost gone, except in some pretentious establishments that aspire to *haute cuisine* but lack the skills to produce it.

There is a new confidence in cooking. Fashions have been taken up, followed and rejected, and now an eclectic atmosphere prevails. Replacing the stylized 'every plate a picture', cuisine is now cooking that draws on classic origins but combines bourgeois and ethnic flavours and techniques, and is presented by each chef in his or her own style.

The chefs we met in the first two series of *Take Six Cooks*, who set the gastronomic scene in Britain in the last five years, are now well-respected, establishment figures – Anton Mosimann, Albert and Michel Roux, Pierre Koffmann, Raymond Blanc and Nico Ladenis. You'll find their direct influence on at least two of the chefs in this book. In this, the third series of *Take Six Cooks*, our six chefs reflect the current mood in cooking – their cuisine is very individual, very honest and, of course, very good!

In this book we have asked the chefs to contribute recipes not only for their course in the series but for the other five courses as well. So each chef has contributed fifteen or so recipes which we think will give you more idea of the different cooking styles.

We are pleased to include **Michel Bourdin**, *Chef de Cuisine* at the Connaught Hotel in London since 1975, and President of the Académie Culinaire in Britain since it was founded on 6th December 1980. Michel's course is hors d'oeuvres and you'll find that many of his recipes are almost culinary history lessons. The Terrine Connaught and Game Pie date back many years and this is the first time the recipes have been made public. The ingredients alone for Game Pie make us realise how lucky we are in this country to have access to so many varieties of game; nowhere else in the world could this dish be made! At the Connaught Hotel, Michel has translated traditional British dishes into *haute cuisine*. Roast beef and Yorkshire pudding lovers please note his recipe on page 20.

For soups and sauces we have selected **Marco Pierre White**, who has worked for many of the people we have met in the first two series of *Take Six Cooks* – Albert Roux, Pierre Koffman, Nico Ladenis and Raymond Blanc. Every recipe you read from Marco is the result of a long process of distillation of what he has learned from the best kitchens in the land – a concentrated reduction if you like of the very best advice he could be given, plus, of course, his own hallmark. The results are stunning.

The fish course belongs to **Gunn Eriksen**, and there can't be many cooks who have their own fish larder outside the back door, under the sea! Gunn's Norwegian roots, her love of things wild, and her detachment from the 'foodie circuit' show clearly in her choices and her style. Wolf-fish, bittercress, ground elder and nettles are new flavours to challenge the more prosaic turbot, parsley and chives.

Welsh Lamb with a Garlic Sauce **Franco Taruschio** PAGE 77

For vegetables we have turned to **Paul Gayler**, who has introduced, as far as we know, the first *Menu Potager* into a restaurant of the class of Inigo Jones in London. His vegetable dishes are as rich as meat or fish courses, but they are clever, balanced, delicious and incredibly pretty.

We have gone to Wales to the Walnut Tree in Abergavenny for our meat courses – where **Franco Taruschio** has been delighting people for twenty-five years with his food. He combines Italian, Welsh and Thai themes very happily in his cooking, and you'll find them all reflected in his selection of recipes. His Welsh lamb is not so very different from *Arosto d'Abbacchio* – a feast-day dish in Italy – and his lasagne has only been adjusted to meet the British preference for meat over pasta.

Robert Mey of the Hyatt Carlton Tower in London is our pâtissier of the series. With forty years' experience, Robert has seen fashions come and go – and with the confidence of a man who has seen it all, he is happy to include Crème Brûlée and Brioche Pudding with the more current flavours like Nougat Glacé.

Undoubtedly, in the last few years there have been pressures on chefs to change their styles – often I think to provide a new angle, fresh copy for the food writers (and what a lot of twaddle is written about food!). However, the climate is becoming apposite for many more British chefs to take their place among the best of the French chefs. Who knows, in the next series of *Take Six Cooks* all our chefs might be English!

Enjoy reading the recipes and even if, as in the Connaught Game Pie, you never get round to making it, you'll surely appreciate the labour, yes, of love it obviously is to produce this dish perfectly. So it's worth remembering that whatever you cook – even if it's an egg or cheese on toast – it can be done well, presented carefully. It takes very little extra time and yet makes such a difference.

Michel Bourdin

If you are lunching at the Connaught on a Monday you can be sure of Steak, Kidney and Mushroom Pie; if it's Tuesday, Irish Stew; and on Wednesday it's always Roast Beef and Yorkshire Pudding. This insistence on tradition is what makes the Connaught one of the more enduring institutions in British life. Ninety per cent of its guests are regular and many of the 280 staff have been in the same job for twenty years or more.

The Connaught motto, '*Placere Placet*' – 'the pleasure to please', has ensured that the tution is more important then the individuals who work there, which suits Michel Bourdin very well. 'The Connaught is the star,' he says, and he is content to preserve a little mystique as its *Chef de Cuisine*. It was the Connaught's sense of history and tradition rather than the desire to be in England that persuaded Michel to head the kitchens in 1975. 'Tradition will always be fashionable. Fashions change. Few become traditions.' So Michel didn't mind that the menu at the Connaught, though printed every day, was pretty firmly fixed even in its daily variations. But didn't this make Michel a prisoner of the Connaught repertoire? 'Not at all . . . To achieve a standard is one thing but to maintain that standard is another – and that was the challenge.' Michel's parents ran a *bar/tabac* in Paris and sent Michel on a food and management course at the local cookery school, hoping he would take over the business. But while his college friends were busy turning into managers, Michel decided to cook, and found himself a humble *commis* in the kitchen along with 13- and 14-year-olds. Even after he married Mereille, and they had moved to Maxim's in Paris, she earned more as a waitress there than he did in the kitchen.

However, as the Connaught is to London, so Maxim's is to Paris and Michel was very happy moving through the ranks under the special eye of Alex Humbert, the *Chef de Cuisine*, who became Michel's mentor. 'He was the man who could reconcile nouvelle and *ancien* cuisine,' and from him Michel learned that 'when you cook you have to give a little bit of yourself'. Ironically, Michel often cooked dishes at Maxim's that came from the Connaught – like bread sauce for roast meat, and bread and butter pudding and rice pudding too – so when he was recommended for the job at the Connaught he had a clue what to expect.

Fifty chefs are now employed in the kitchen and at first Michel made a deliberate effort to engineer a 100 per cent British brigade. It just didn't work; the chemistry was wrong, the motivation lacking. So now, the ratio is 80:20, with mostly Europeans making up the 20 per cent. Michel is a passionate European, believing that British chefs must unite with those in France to preserve the purity of French cuisine. 'If we don't protect this culinary identity we will have to go to Japan, who reproduce everything so well, or to America, who have all the money. To keep our culinary heritage in Europe we must join forces.' However, Michel thinks we still have ten years at least to wait before British chefs will be able to cook British food as well as the French do, but he does concede that 'as Escoffier wrote his classic guide in England – it is through Britain that the world has been influenced'. It's odd to hear British dishes like Oxtail or Steak and Kidney Pie being called for at the service in broken English, but decidedly refreshing to see best-quality produce simply cooked – like English asparagus served with melted butter, or a mixed grill that didn't pretend to be anything more than it was. And there were no raised eyebrows either at an order for sausages with a béarnaise sauce. 'Customers have the last word – they are the ones who dictate style. The chef proposes; the customer disposes.'

The guests at the Connaught love the silver service. 'Our food is presented twice – first in its silver dish and then when it has been served – and it has to look good both times.' Game has been a speciality for years. In season there is teal, woodcock, grouse, pheasant, partridge (strictly grey leg not red, of course – although frankly Michel suspects there is very little difference in the flavour) hare, venison and wild duck. Most of it comes from Allens, the 'film set' aristocratic butcher's shop, a stone's throw from the Connaught. The hotel's famous Game Pie uses all eight types of game and the Terrine Connaught is a dish that dates back thirty years. Pork, both lean and fat, foie gras, duck or pheasant and a clarified game jelly make up this recipe which Bocuse uses in his restaurant. Michel believes terrrines are the hallmark, the stamp, of any chef.

The Connaught guests eat pluckily through 800 kg/364 lb of foie gras every year – which costs £17.85 a portion at present prices; Beluga caviar is now £51.80 for 50 g/2oz; and as for truffles, a strong cold box in the kitchen holds £50,000-worth; that's more than they keep in the safe upstairs. The psychological security these ingredients give people who eat them equably balances the financial security the hotel itself enjoys. Michel Bourdin has his theories about the British public: 'They are all genuine in their tastes – honest and unpretentious – but oh dear you all suffer from an island complex.' The British are afraid to explore anything new – either because we don't think it could possibly match the old, or we are too afraid of finding anything better.

He cares very deeply about his young chefs. He doesn't believe the path he followed is right; it is far better for a boy to work an apprenticeship with a day release to college to combine theory with experience. Michel takes on two youngsters every year at the Connaught and insists that their parents are present at the interviews. He doesn't cloud the issues – in his opinion it takes ten to fifteen years to become a chef. The first ten years are spent learning the craft and the other four or five developing a personal style; so it takes far longer than to become a doctor, dentist or lawyer. Too many people try to cut corners, and it shows. A wide secure base is needed for a pyramid of excellence if one is not to waver at the top.

Michael's culinary foundations are solid – indeed the august body of the Académie Culinaire of France created a precedent when they voted Michel and J. Robuchon into their organization seven years ahead of time – when Michel was only twenty-eight. That was in 1968. One hundred and three years after being founded in France, on 6th December 1980, a branch of the Académie Culinaire was opened in Britain. With Michel Bourdin as president and the titular head, there are now over a hundred members whose aim it is to maintain the highest standards in French and British cuisine, and to improve training and conditions. Ultimately it is hoped to found an academy – a university of culinary art – to ensure classical principles will never give way to gimmicky fads, or creativity to self-indulgence.

All this will please Michel Bourdin. He is a man who is very proud of his profession – of its traditions, of its classical style; it's an honourable craft he doesn't want to see in the hands of cowboys – so-called star chefs who are in fact charlatans. One of his sons, Charles, is now training at his old college in France and Michel has told him: 'Cooking is a way of giving and of making yourself desirable, so do it simply and unelaborately and you will do well.'

Crème Cyro's

A Soup of Mussels and Cream

This is from the famous restaurant Cyro's in Deauville, where it was created in the 1920s.

•

SERVES 8
6 l/10 ½ pt mussels
2 onions
1 head of celery
bouquet garni (parsley, thyme and bay leaf)
1 soupsp white peppercorns
½ small head of garlic
¼ bottle dry white wine
3 l/5 ¼ pt chicken stock
900 ml/1 ½ pt double cream
cayenne pepper
salt

•

1 Scrape and wash the mussels thoroughly, removing the beards. Discard any that are broken or open and do not shut when tapped.
2 Slice the onions and celery sticks and put them in a very large, deep saucepan with the bouquet garni, white peppercorns and garlic.
3 Add the mussels with the wine and enough chicken stock to three-quarters cover the mussels.
4 Cook with the lid on, tossing the pan from time to time, until the mussels open.
5 Strain off the liquid, return it to the pan and boil the liquid until reduced by a quarter.
6 Bring the cream to the boil in a separate pan and reduce it until slightly thickened and then add to the mussel liquid. Adjust the seasoning to taste with cayenne pepper and salt.
7 This soup can be served with cheese straws, or it is equally nice cold.

The mussels used in this recipe can be served cold as an hors d'oeuvre with a sauce rémoulade. This is a basic mayonnaise (made with corn oil and white wine vinegar) to which more Dijon mustard has been added together with chopped capers, gherkins, parsley and *fine herbes*.

Sauce Pudeur

This sauce was created during my time at Maxim's Rue Royal. It should be served with my creation *Pâté de Turbot Froid au Homard*. The name *Pudeur*, 'prude' in English, reflects the pinkish colour of the sauce which is similar to the colour of the cheeks of a blushing lady.

•

1 tbsp tomato ketchup
200 ml/7 fl oz whipped cream

•

MAYONNAISE
3 egg yolks
2 tsp Dijon mustard
600 ml/1 pt corn oil
1 tbsp white wine vinegar
salt and pepper

•

COULIS OF TOMATOES
3 medium tomatoes, peeled and de-seeded
1 onion, chopped
bouquet garni
1 clove of garlic, crushed
2 tbsp tomato purée

•

1 To make the mayonnaise, lightly mix the egg yolks with the mustard and then gradually add the corn oil and beat until it thickens. Add the white wine vinegar and season.
2 To make the coulis of tomatoes, chop the tomatoes into a pan along with the chopped onion, bouquet garni, garlic and tomato purée. Cook until soft. Liquidize the mixture and then sieve it to make the coulis.
3 Add the coulis to the mayonnaise, and a little ketchup for colour.
4 Lightly whip the cream to a ribbon consistency and add to the sauce. Serve with cold fish dishes.

Salade de Fonds d'Artichauts et Champignons aux Crustaces 'Aphrodite' PAGE 13

Game Pie du Chef

This is a mosaic – a symphony of taste and colour achieved by alternating a red farce of game and pork with white game strips and a white farce of game and pork with red game strips. As you will see, it is out of the question for you to reproduce it exactly – but if you have access to game, perhaps by scaling down the quantities you can achieve your own Game Pie du Maison.

•

SERVES 12–14

•

RED MEAT
4 grouse
2 wild duck
2 widgeon
1 snipe
2 black cock
4 plover
1 hare
1 chump end of venison

•

RED MARINADE
500 ml/18 fl oz Maderia
200 ml/7 fl oz fine champagne (V.S.O.P.)
25 g/1 oz salt per 1 kg/2 ¼ lb meat

•

WHITE MEAT
2 guinea fowl
2 domestic duck
4 pheasant
6 partridge
3 quails
300 g/11 oz ham
300 g/11 oz veal
300 g/11 oz chicken

•

WHITE MARINADE
500 ml/18 fl oz Muscadet
a dash of Pernod or Ricard, or similar
100 g/3 ½ oz shallots (cooked in enough white wine to cover)
250 ml/9 fl oz olive oil
25 g/1 oz salt per 1 kg/2 ¼ lb meat

GARNISH
whole pistachio nuts
batonets of truffle
batonets of semi-cooked foie gras
wild mushrooms (oyster mushrooms, pieds de mouton etc), seasoned, cooked and drained

•

RED FARCE (OR STUFFING)
1 kg/2 ¼ lb game meat (red flesh)
500 g/1 lb 2 oz pork meat
900 g/2 lb flair (pork fat from belly)
300 g/11 oz farce à gratin (sautéed livers of chicken, black cock and grouse, mixed with back fat of pork and foie gras)
15 g/ ½ oz spiced salt per 1 kg/2 ¼ lb meat

•

WHITE FARCE (OR STUFFING)
900 g/2 lb game meat (white flesh)
400 g/14 oz pork, veal and chicken
700 g/1 ½ lb flair (pork fat from belly)
15 g/ ½ oz spiced salt per 1 kg/2 ¼ lb meat

•

GAME GELÉE
bones of red and white game
bones of pork
85 g/3 oz mirepoix (onions, carrots and garlic)
beef stock
egg whites for clarifying

•

1 Cut all the meat into thin strips (aiguillettes) and place in the appropriate marinade for at least 24 hours.
2 Next day, mix the ingredients for the stuffings and put through a fine mincer twice (keeping the red and white separate).
3 Put each into a food processor with the appropriate marinade that has been drained from the aiguillettes. Keep the stuffings cool in separate containers in the refrigerator.
4 To make the game gelée, use the same method as for the Terrine Connaught (see recipe on page 16): roast the bones of red and white game and the bones of pork with the mirepoix of vegetables, then cover with beef stock and simmer for

4–5 hours. Clarify as you would for consommé by whisking the egg whites into the stock, then pouring the liquid through muslin or a fine sieve. The impurities should be caught in the egg white. This stock should set into a strong game *gelée*.

5 Mould the game pie: using a large pie dish, start the mosaic with a layer of the white stuffing.

6 Next add a layer of red *aiguillettes*, alternating them with the garnish of pistachios, truffle, foie gras and wild mushrooms.

7 The next layer should be red stuffing.

8 White *aiguillettes* should now be laid over the red stuffing, along with pistachios, wild mushrooms, truffles and foie gras, alternating as in the previous layer.

9 Add white stuffing on top of this, and continue in this way until finished. Always finish with a layer of stuffing.

10 Cover the pie dish with the *pâte à pâte* (see below), and cook in the oven at 190°C/375°F/Gas Mark 5 for about 1¾ hours.

11 Let the pie cool gently, adding some of the *gelée* while it is still warm. Inject this into the body of the pie. The remaining *gelée* should be added when the pie is completely cold. It can be cut into little dice and served beside the pie or used to glaze the pie to prevent oxidation.

•

PÂTE À PÂTE
This is a special rich pastry.

•

250 g/9 oz flour
70 g/2 ½ oz butter
1 egg, beaten
a large pinch of salt
water to mix

•

1 Mix the ingredients to a dough as you would for shortcrust pastry. Leave to rest in the refrigerator for at least 30 minutes.

2 Roll out and use to cover the pie dish (see above).

Salade de Fonds d'Artichauts et Champignons aux Crustaces 'Aphrodite'

Artichoke and Mushroom Salad with a Garnish of Shellfish

This owes its name to the addition of the black truffle from Périgord known as the black diamond and renowned for its aphrodisiac qualities.

•

SERVES 1
1 artichoke bottom
blanc de légumes (boiling water with 1 tbsp flour and a squeeze of lemon juice added)
40 g/1 ½ oz large button mushrooms
10 g/¼ oz truffle and a little truffle oil
lemon juice
salt and pepper
a few leaves of radicchio and frisée lettuce and some vinaigrette
1 soupsp white crabmeat
2 slices of cooked lobster
2 langoustines, cut lengthways
2 écrevisses
sprigs of chervil

•

1 Cook the artichoke bottom in the *blanc de légumes* for 8–10 minutes.

2 Cut the mushrooms on the cross into large pieces. Slice the truffle into julienne strips.

3 Cut the artichoke bottom into large pieces while still warm and add to the mushrooms, with a squeeze of lemon juice, a little truffle oil and some of the julienne strips of truffle. Allow to infuse for a few minutes. Season to taste.

4 Prepare the salad leaves and toss in vinaigrette at the last minute. Arrange on a plate. Put the artichoke and mushroom mixture in the centre.

5 Steam the crustacea – the crab, lobster, langoustines and écrevisses – for a few minutes to warm through, season well and place on top.

6 Garnish with a few julienne strips of truffle and a few sprigs of chervil.

Terrine Connaught PAGE 16

Petits Egg'scellents PAGE 17

Terrine Connaught

This terrine is made with pheasant and woodcock during the game season (October to February) and with duck for the rest of the year.

To achieve a well-balanced terrine, ensure that, of the total weight of lean duck meat, lean pork and flair (pork fat from the belly), at least a quarter is lean duck meat and at least one-third is flair.

At the Connaught, we cook up to ten terrines at a time – I cannot guarantee that using smaller quantities you will achieve the results we do there, but in the spirit of the Terrine Connaught, here is a domestic recipe.

•

SERVES AT LEAST 12
1 duck (300 g/11 oz duck meat)
65–70 ml/2 ½ fl oz port
25 ml/1 fl oz brandy
1 tbsp rum
1 soupsp salt
1 tsp freshly ground pepper
a large pinch of quatre épices
a large pinch of saltpetre
a large pinch of sel rose
525 g/1 lb 3 oz pork
450 g/1 lb pork flair
20 g/¾ oz batonets of truffle
125 g/4 ½ oz batonets of foie gras (semi-cooked)
25 g/1 oz pistachio nuts

•

STOCK
duck bones and skin
85 g/3 oz mirepoix (onion, carrot and garlic)
pork bones
900 ml/1 ½ pt good beef stock

•

GARNISH
bay leaves
sprigs of thyme

•

1 Allow three days to make this recipe. On the first day, bone the duck, keeping the breasts separate – you need 300 g/11 oz of duck meat. Make sure the meat is free of all sinews.

2 Trim and cut the duck breasts into *aiguillettes* (thin strips as deep as they are wide but varying in length). Marinate in the port, brandy and a dash of the rum mixed with the seasonings. Leave for 24 hours.

3 To make the stock, chop the duck bones and put with the skin in a baking tray. Roast in the oven together with the *mirepoix* of onions, carrots and garlic at 220°C/425°F/Gas Mark 7 for 30–40 minutes.

4 Trim the pork of fat and remove the bones. Add the pork bones and skin to the duck bones and skin in the oven to roast until brown.

5 Add the beef stock and cook slowly over a low heat for 4–6 hours. Pass the stock through a sieve, keeping back the bones – it should yield 600 ml/1 pt. Leave in a cool place to set into a strong *gelée*.

6 Place the roasted duck and pork bones in a saucepan, add enough water to cover, and bring to the boil. Skim, simmer for 4–6 hours, then pass through a sieve. Return the stock to the pan and cook until reduced to a syrupy *glace de viande* – you need 60 ml/2 fl oz.

7 Clean the pork flair of all its sinews.

8 Pass the lean pork and the same quantity of flair through a mincer (using a medium-large hole). Make sure there is equal distribution of flair to pork in the mixture.

9 With the mincer on a medium hole, pass the duck meat through, using a little flair at the end to work through.

10 Mix the minced pork and duck with the remainder of the marinade and leave for 24 hours.

11 Next day, heat the basic stock, allow to cool and then add to it the *glace de viande* to melt it.

12 Add the stock to the mixture of pork, duck and flair and stir, but don't overwork. Put the mixture in the refrigerator with a few truffle peelings overnight.

13 On the third day, test the mixture for seasoning – fry a little in a pan and taste. Adjust seasoning if necessary.

14 Take an earthenware or porcelain terrine mould – its sides should be at least 1 cm/½ in thick – and place some of the meat mixture in the bottom.

15 Use the strips of marinated duck, truffle, foie gras and whole pistachios to make the second layer.

16 Add another layer of the mixture and then another layer of duck strips, truffle, foie gras and pistachios.

17 Finish with a layer of mixture and put ½ bay leaf and a sprig of thyme on top of the terrine. (If you have mixture over, make another terrine and cook it to put in the freezer, or cook and seal for later use and keep in the refrigerator.)

18 Put the terrine into a bain-marie (containing warm water) and cook covered in foil in the oven at 180°C/350°F/Gas Mark 4 for 1 ½ hours. Make sure the cooking tray is turned during this time to allow even cooking throughout.

19 Remove the foil 10 minutes before the end, to allow the terrine to colour slightly.

20 Remove the terrine from the oven and add the remaining rum to it while still warm. Apply weights to the terrine for a while; take them off just before it is completely cold.

Petits Egg'scellents

These are crisp pastry boats filled with scrambled egg, diced truffle, quails' eggs and hollandaise sauce.

•

SERVES 4
100 g/3 ½ oz puff pastry
8 eggs
16 quails' eggs
salt and pepper
50 g/2 oz butter
a little double cream (optional)
25 g/1 oz truffle, diced and kept in its own juice
julienne strips of truffle and sprigs of chervil for garnish

HOLLANDAISE SAUCE
1 tbsp water
1–2 egg yolks
85 g/3 oz unsalted butter
juice of ¼ lemon
cayenne pepper
salt

•

1 Mould the puff pastry into eight boat-shaped moulds and cook in the oven at 220°C/425°F/Gas Mark 7 until golden – about 10 minutes. Allow two boats per person.

2 Make the hollandaise sauce: whisk the water and egg yolks in a double saucepan until the mixture is creamy and the whisk leaves a trail on the bottom of the pan. Do not overheat. Take off the heat and beat in the butter, a little at a time. Finish with lemon juice, cayenne pepper and salt to taste.

3 Break the eggs into a mixing bowl, season with salt and pepper, and mix lightly.

4 Warm the diced truffle in a little of its own liquor, then drain it.

5 Heat a thick-bottomed saucepan and add the butter to warm – don't allow it to get too hot – then add the eggs, stirring all the time. (If the eggs are cooking too quickly, add a little cream off the heat to stop the cooking process – the eggs must be kept soft.) When the eggs are almost cooked, add the warm truffle.

6 Fill the pastry boats with the scrambled eggs and truffle.

7 Boil the quails' eggs so that they are *mollet* (soft-boiled) – 1 ½–2 minutes. Peel them, and place 2 eggs on top of each boat and season lightly.

8 Coat each egg with a soupspoonful of hollandaise sauce.

9 Garnish each boat with julienne strips of truffle and a sprig of chervil.

Michel Bourdin

Kipper Pâté PAGE 19

Kipper Pâté

SERVES 12 AS AN HORS D'OEUVRE
1.25 kg/2 ½ lb kippers, grilled, boned and skinned
550 g/1 ¼ lb onions, sliced
350 g/12 oz back bacon
450 g/1 lb potatoes, cooked in their jackets
3 eggs
salt and pepper
quatres épices
whisky and Drambuie to taste
pork flair (pork fat from the belly) to cover the pâté

•

1 Sweat the onions and bacon in a covered pan until the onions are transparent and soft. Cool slightly.

2 Peel the cooked potatoes, cut into quarters and add to the onions and bacon.

3 Add the flaked kipper to the mixture and then pass it all through a coarse-hole mincer.

4 Mix the eggs, seasonings and alcohol to taste, and beat to a fluffy batter mix.

5 Mix the kipper with the egg mixture and place it in a terrine mould.

6 Cook over hot water in a bain-marie in the oven at 180°C/350°F/Gas Mark 4 for 45–50 minutes, but halfway through cooking allow the mixture to rest (so the eggs won't rise) for about 5 minutes, and then continue cooking.

7 When the terrine is cold, melt the pork flair in a pan and pour over the terrine. This helps to preserve the flavour and allows it to be stored without spoiling.

Paillard de Saumon d'Écosse 'Jean Troisgros'

Escalope of Salmon Served with a Sorrel Sauce

This dish has been reproduced at the Connaught in memory of a dear friend, Jean, from the Troisgros family. Our profession will sadly miss this great chef.

•

SERVES 1
150 g/5 oz Scottish salmon
salt and pepper
2 shallots
100 ml/3 ½ fl oz Noilly Prat
475 ml/16 fl oz fish stock
100 ml/3 ½ fl oz double cream
a handful of fresh sorrel
fresh lemon juice
sprigs of chervil for garnish

•

1 Cut the *paillard* (a thin but wide escalope of salmon) from the middle of the salmon. Very gently flatten it out between layers of clingfilm.

2 Season with salt and pepper and then dry-cook it quickly in a non-stick pan. Set aside in a warm place.

3 Finely chop the shallots and put in a pan with the Noilly Prat and fish stock. Bring to the boil and cook until reduced by half. Pass the mixture through a sieve to remove the shallots.

4 Return the liquid to the heat, add the cream and boil again until reduced to the consistency of a thick pouring sauce.

5 Cut the sorrel into thin strips – *chiffonades* – and add to the sauce. Adjust the seasoning. Add a dash of lemon juice just before serving to boost the flavour.

6 Spread the sauce on the plate. Place the salmon carefully on top and garnish with chervil.

Bar Roche 'Christian Dior'

Baked Sea Bass in a Breadcrumb and Egg Coating

This recipe was created for Christian Dior – one of our famous Parisian gourmets.

•

SERVES 1

1 × 450-g/1-lb sea bass
salt and pepper
a mirepoix of 50 g/2 oz each of onions, celery and shallots
1 clove of garlic
bouquet garni (loose)
70 ml/2 ½ fl oz white wine
70 ml/2 ½ fl oz fish stock
70 ml/2 ½ fl oz white chicken stock
40 g/1 ½ oz fresh breadcrumbs
50 g/2 oz butter
2 hard-boiled eggs
2 tbsp chopped parsley
a few capers

•

BEURRE FONDU

85 ml/3 fl oz boiling water
75 g/2 ¾ oz soft butter
fine herbes
a dash of Pernod

•

1 Keeping the head and tail intact, with a sharp knife *ciseler* (make little nicks in) the skin of the fish and season.
2 Put the *mirepoix* of vegetables, the garlic and bouquet garni in a baking tray with enough liquid to come up to but not touch the fish as it rests on a cooling tray or trivet above it. The fish should be half roasted and half steamed using this method.
3 Protect the head and tail during cooking by wrapping them in foil. Cook in a preheated oven at 200°C/400°C/Gas Mark 6 for 20–30 minutes. Baste frequently with the cooking liquor – the skin should be moist but slightly golden.
4 Fry the breadcrumbs in a little of the butter until brown. Drain on kitchen paper until dry.

5 Make the *beurre fondu*: to the boiling water add the soft butter, a little at a time. Finally, add a few *fines herbes* and a dash of Pernod.
6 Chop the hard-boiled egg whites and yolks separately (this is known as mimosa).
7 Heat a little more butter in the frying pan until it is nutty colour (*beurre noisette*), then toss the fried breadcrumbs in it and add almost all the mimosa and 1 tablespoon of chopped parsley.
8 When the fish is cooked, place on a plate and cover the body with the breadcrumb mixture (leaving the head and tail free from crumbs).
9 Toss a few capers in a little more *beurre noisette* and pour these over the fish.
10 Garnish with the remaining mimosa and chopped parsley. Serve with the *beurre fondu*.

Roast Sirloin of Scottish Beef Cooked on the Bone

a good sirloin on the bone (up to 4.5 kg/10 lb)
beef dripping (just enough to cover baking tray)
salt and pepper
beef bones and trimmings (previously roasted)
a mirepoix of 1 carrot, 1 onion, 2 sticks of celery and 1 clove of garlic
115 g/4 oz butter

•

YORKSHIRE PUDDING

4 eggs
225 g/8 oz plain flour
300 ml/ ½ pt milk
salt and pepper
a little nutmeg
a little beef dripping

•

1 Melt the beef dripping in a baking tray to coat the base. Season the meat well and place it, fat uppermost, in the hot dripping.
2 Cook in the oven at 220°C/425°C/Gas Mark 7, allowing about 10 minutes per 450 g/1 lb for rare meat, 15 minutes for medium-rare meat, and 20 minutes for meat well done. Baste frequently.

3 Place the beef bones and trimmings in a roasting pan with the *mirepoix* and 900 ml/1 ½ pt water. Simmer for 2–6 hours until reduced by one-third; you should have 600 ml/1pt of *jus de boeuf*.

4 When the joint is cooked, remove it from the pan and keep it warm. Deglaze the pan with half the *jus de boeuf* – this is the gravy.

5 Reduce the remaining *jus de boeuf* to about 2 tablespoons of *glace de viande*, a syrupy final reduction. Coat the joint of meat with this beef jelly and some butter which has been heated to the brown nutty stage (*beurre noisette*).

6 To make the Yorkshire pudding, mix together the eggs and flour and then gradually add the milk and seasoning. Beat lightly to a batter.

7 Heat the beef dripping and add a little to the batter. Use the rest to line tartlet trays – to take individual Yorkshire puddings. Place a little batter in each compartment and put in the oven at 200°C/400°C/Gas Mark 6. After 10 minutes, lower the heat to 180°C/350°F/Gas Mark 4 for the remaining 10 minutes' cooking time.

Tourte de Perdreau de Chasse aux Diamants

Partridge Pie with a Sauce of Truffles

•

SERVES 4
4 wild partridges
salt and pepper
1 Savoy cabbage
25 g/1 oz truffle and a little truffle oil
50 g/2 oz semi-cooked foie gras (tinned)
225 g/8 oz puff pastry
water or a little beaten egg for egg wash

•

SAUCE PÉRIGUEUX
300 ml/ ½ pt light veal stock
25 ml/1 fl oz Madeira
a few chopped truffles
300 ml/ ½ pt stock made from partridge bones
added to veal stock

1 Using only wild partridges, season them and roast *à la goutte de sang* (undercooked so that when the breast is punctured with a needle a pearl of blood appears) in the oven at 220°C/425°F/Gas Mark 7 – about 7 minutes.

2 Allow the partridges to cool and then divide them into supremes, keeping the breast and thigh intact but removing the drumstick. (The drumsticks can be used as a cold hors d'oeuvre.) All the bones will go to make the partridge stock.

3 Blanch 4 good cabbage leaves large enough to form envelopes in boiling salted water. Refresh.

4 Cook the heart of the cabbage in boiling water for about 5 minutes. Drain and chop into small pieces, enough to stuff the 4 leaves. Flavour this filling with a little truffle oil and some of the truffle, cut into julienne strips. Adjust the seasoning.

5 Wrap the filling in the cabbage leaves to form small filled envelopes.

6 Cut the supremes diagonally in half. Place two supremes for each person side by side to make a heart shape. Place the envelopes of cabbage and julienne strips of truffle in the middle.

7 Roll out the puff pastry into four squares large enough to encase the partridge. Place a layer of semi-cooked foie gras, cut very thinly, on the pastry, reserving another layer for the top. Add a few julienne strips of truffle and place the partridge and cabbage on top. Cover with a second layer of foie gras and truffle. Season well.

8 Mould the pastry around the filling. Brush the pastry with water or lightly egg-wash to ensure it sticks together. Allow to rest in the refrigerator for a few hours before cooking.

9 Cook in the oven at 200°C/400°F/Gas Mark 6 to start with for 8–10 minutes, and then turn down to 180°C/350°F/Gas Mark 4 for another 8–10 minutes.

10 Serve the partridge with the Sauce Périgueux – made from basic Périgueux (the veal stock reduced by one-third with the Madeira and truffles) mixed with the partridge stock.

Accompany with three purées: pea, celeriac and chestnut.

Fonds d'Artichauts Princesse

Artichokes with Asparagus in a Mornay Sauce

•

SERVES 4
2 artichokes
12 asparagus spears
blanc de légumes (boiling water with 1 tbsp flour
and a squeeze of lemon juice added)
salt and pepper
50 g/2 oz butter
1 soupsp Jersey cream
Parmesan cheese for topping

•

MORNAY SAUCE
20 g/ ¾ oz butter
20 g/ ¾ oz flour
225 ml/8 fl oz milk
1 egg yolk
175 g/6 oz Gruyère cheese, grated
salt and pepper

•

1 Cook the artichokes in the *blanc de légumes* for 8–10 minutes.
2 Cook the asparagus spears in boiling salted water and cool them down over ice so they keep their colour when cold.
3 Cut the artichoke bottoms on the cross and sauté them in the just melting butter. Add the Jersey cream, season to taste, and warm gently until thickened.
4 Cover the bottom of a serving dish with the artichokes, which should be lightly coated with the cream.
5 Quickly warm up the asparagus spears and place them on top.
6 To make the mornay sauce, melt the butter in a saucepan, add the flour and cook gently until golden. Off the heat, add the milk a little at a time. Return to the heat and add the egg yolk and the grated Gruyère cheese. Stir until a good consistency, then season.
7 Cover the artichoke and asparagus mixture with the mornay sauce, top with Parmesan cheese and put under the grill until brown.

Pommes Soufflées 'Arlequin'

'Harlequin' Soufflé Potatoes

It is important to use the appropriate potatoes when making this dish: Maris Piper Q.V. or New Cyprus or Pentland Crown.

•

potatoes, peeled and cut into 3-mm/ ⅛-in slices
vegetable oil (not new)
salt

•

1 Shape the slices of potatoes in different ways – triangles, pillow shapes, flowers with a hole in the middle, ovals etc.
2 Bring a large pan of vegetable oil (which has been used before) to a temperature of about 180°C/350°F and cook the potato shapes slightly without colouring them too much. Once the potatoes have been added to the oil, the temperature will drop, so bring back to the correct heat. (Old oil is better because it does not reach the very high temperatures that new oil does.) Drain on kitchen paper.
3 Cook for the second time in purer oil (at 170°C/340°F), which will make the potatoes puff up as the air imprisoned in them tries to escape. At this stage, they can be stored on non-stick paper in the refrigerator until required.
4 To serve, toss the potatoes back into very hot oil (180°C/350°F) and allow them to puff up once more and to crisp to hold their shape. Remove from the oil, dry on kitchen paper, season with salt and serve immediately.

Crêpes Madame De . . .

Madame De . . . is one of the most popular titles of Louise de Vilmorin. The heroines of the book, set at the end of the last century, revelled in the sensual pleasures of life – one of which was undoubtedly good food.

•

SERVES 6

•

CRÊPES (MAKES 12)
250 g/9 oz plain flour
2 whole eggs
2 egg yolks
475 ml/16 fl oz milk
150 g/5 oz butter

•

FILLING
115 g/4 oz candied pineapple, diced
50 ml/2 fl oz Cointreau
300 ml/½ pt crème pâtissière
(see below)
200 ml/7 fl oz whipping cream
200 g/7 oz granulated sugar

•

CRÈME PÂTISSIÈRE
300 ml/½ pt milk
100 g/3 ½ oz caster sugar
3 eggs
25 g/1 oz cornflour

•

1 Soak the candied pineapple in the Cointreau for at least 30 minutes. Drain. Set the liqueur aside.
2 Make the crêpes: make a well in the flour, add the beaten eggs, egg yolks and milk, and stir until well mixed.
3 Heat the butter until it sizzles and begins to turn brown (*beurre noisette*), then whisk into the crêpe mixture. Leave to rest for at least 30 minutes.
4 When you cook the crêpes, you will not need oil in the pan (the fat is already incorporated in the crêpes). Cook them in advance and allow to cool.
5 Prepare the *crème pâtissière*: heat the milk with half the sugar. Meanwhile, put the eggs in a bowl with the remaining sugar and beat well, then add the cornflour.
6 When the milk is boiling, pour half into the egg and sugar mixture and then pour the mixture back into the boiling milk. Stir over a gentle heat until thickened. Allow to cool.
7 Whip the cream and mix with the cooled *crème pâtissière*. Add the drained pineapple. Fill the crêpes with this mixture and fold in two.
8 Take a fireproof or stainless steel dish, large enough to hold 12 folded crêpes, butter it lightly and sprinkle with most of the sugar. Put it over a high heat to caramelize until golden. Add a few drops of Cointreau to the pan.
9 Put the filled crêpes into the pan, sprinkle with the rest of the sugar and brown under the grill.
10 Warm the remaining Cointreau, flame it and pour over the crêpes. Serve immediately – two crêpes per person.

Lemon Posset

SERVES 4
3 large lemons
900 ml/1 ½ pt double cream
150 g/5 oz caster sugar
24 raspberries

•

1 Peel the zest from the lemons. Squeeze the juice from the lemons and place in a separate bowl.
2 Place the lemon zest, double cream, and sugar in a thick-bottomed pan and bring to the boil.
3 When boiling, pour the mixture over the lemon juice and mix very lightly together. Place the bowl on ice to cool it quickly.
4 Put the raspberries either into individual glasses or into one large glass dish.
5 While the mixture is still just warm, cover the fruit with some of it and let it set in the refrigerator for about 15 minutes.
6 When this mixture is set, add the rest of the mixture until just below the top of the glasses or dish. Leave to set in the refrigerator overnight.
7 Serve very cold.

Marco Pierre White

'My neck is on the block, my career is on the line now I'm on my own', confided Marco Pierre White within months of opening his own restaurant, Harvey's, near Wandsworth Common in South London.

Having worked in the kitchens of most of Britain's top chefs – Albert Roux, Nico Ladenis, Raymond Blanc and Pierre Koffman – at 25 years old Marco took advantage of a Business Expansion Scheme, borrowed £100,000 and started cooking on his own early in 1987. He is still reeling from the press he has already received.

'The discovery of an exceptional new restaurant is of greater importance than a new planet,' says Egon Ronay, justifying an unprecedented half front page article devoted to Marco in *The Sunday Times*. But it's hard to ignore Marco. He's larger than life and urgent for success. 'Today isn't a dress rehearsal for tomorrow,' which is why he reacts so strongly to whatever is happening to him. Whether it's ovens that won't work, or scallops that glisten with freshness, or dogs chasing each other over the common, Marco responds ardently.

Perhaps this highly-charged man has his Italian mother to thank for his zest for living. She died when she was only 39, Marco was just six and his brother only 13 weeks old. They lived in countryside near Genoa in Italy while Marco's father – a Yorkshire businessman – made his money in England. When she died, Marco came to England with his father, leaving his brother in Genoa with childless relatives.

Marco was sent to a grammar school in Harrogate; he was a lonely boy, and the message he received from his headmaster when he left school at 16 was bleak: 'You'll be nothing in life.' However, Marco had one asset – loathe him as some people might, no-one could ignore him.

His next move was logical: 'Everyone who failed in school ended up in catering which is what I did, but it's given me a life-style, a respect, a status, and introductions to people I'd hardly dreamed of.'

I first met Marco when we were filming the second series of *Take Six Cooks* at Le Manoir aux Quat' Saisons near Oxford. Marco was the head chef in Raymond Blanc's absence. Bombastic? Yes. Talented? Certainly. But the indelible impression he left with me was a physical one – a tall thin man with unruly hair, an almost angelic pale face, and arms literally covered with burn scars, present and past. Marco has an almost manic energy. To achieve the results he wants at Harvey's he works 18-hour days, often grabbing a few hours' sleep on a restaurant seat. Even then, his mind isn't still – he dreams about food, he's obsessed by food. 'Through the subtle balance of food', Marco says, 'you can see the balance of life; too much cream or too little can muck up a dish – so too in your life this can happen.' But cooking is a big risk: 'You can never really tell what is going on when the lid is on the sea bass – so many things can go wrong.' Which is why it is, of course, so exciting. Risk means adrenalin, on which Marco fires.

His food is obviously influenced by kitchens in which he has worked, and in the early days of

Harvey's he realised it would be crazy with a staff of only four, all under 24, to serve anything but dishes that were tried and true. 'You can't invent food – but you can put your own hallmark on it.' And that is what Marco is doing. His noisettes of lamb stuffed with a chicken and tarragon mousse, covered with caul, both to keep its shape and to keep it moist during cooking, is an idea from Le Gavroche where Albert Roux used veal and basil instead of lamb and tarragon. A scallop mousse topped with caviar and surrounded by a lattice of leeks is an adaptation of the *tartare de saumon* which Raymond Blanc made famous at Le Manoir. But new dishes are emerging – like calves' brains *en gelée* with asparagus, or a tagliatelle of cockle combs with a fricassee of *girolles*, which Marco is particularly excited about. Just last night he rang ecstatically with news of a new dish: what did I think of a cappucino of lobster? Inwardly I groaned – lobster and coffee? 'No', he said irritably, 'but take the feeling of drinking coffee through the froth of a cappuccino and instead of coffee the liquid would be nage of lobster with little bits of lobster meat which you could sip through a frothy topping of a lobster-flavoured sabayon.' The fact that my mouth was watering as he described it is perhaps proof enough that it could work! But better proof is that when Marco thinks about new dishes it is from a firm classic foundation – from the secure knowledge of what is possible. It's true he hasn't been to college; he did a day release for three weeks and gave it up because what he was learning just didn't seem to bear any relevance to actual work in the kitchen. But Marco is in an enviable position because he has been able to learn from the very best cooks we have in this country – and to take from them all the techniques and the tastes that fit his own philosophy.

Marco has made no-one his master and he is unequivocal about what he won't do. For example, he simply won't don a white jacket bearing his name ('That's all bullshit!'); he won't wear a hat ('They make you itch, then you scratch and what could be worse?'); he won't present food symmetrically on a plate; he won't serve vegetables unless they complement the dish; he won't vacuum-pack fish – he believes the process sucks out the moisture from the fish; he won't cook stocks for long – perhaps 3½ hours for veal and 2½ hours for chicken ('After that the stocks become too salty.'); he won't take the ends off French beans ('One, it's a waste of time, and two, if you do, water gets in during cooking and washes away the goodness as well as the flavour.').

If people coming to Harvey's are guilty of expecting meals of the standard of Le Manoir aux Quat' Saisons for the price of a starter, Marco too is guilty of aspiring to the standards of the places in which he has worked. His cheese board – from Philippe Olivier of Boulogne – makes him no money at all, but professional pride stops him reducing the choice of eleven cheeses. As I watched him carefully unwrap a Reblochon from Beaumont in the Haute Savoie or a Camembert from Normandy, Marco confided that all these places were just names on a map to him. He has never been to France, so has never eaten French three-star food – an irony, certainly, when British food critics are comparing him to the likes of Alain Dutournier and Michel Bras. Marco just chuckles. He relishes the attention, indeed he thrives on it, but above all he's high on the freedom to be himself. 'My boys', as he fondly calls his kitchen staff of four, have already given him a sense of security, a sense perhaps of the family he had and lost. Their dedication is extraordinary: on the job at 8 a.m., no one bothers to go home after lunch, settling instead for a game of football on the common before returning to work for the afternoon. Even at 11.30 p.m. the *mis-en-place* is prepared for the following day.

'But each month – not just my staff – everyone should look in the mirror and ask themselves what they have learned. When you can't answer that question it's time to leave.'

'Life is a gift – life is about balance – but until I'm 80 I'll want to cook and do the service.' Marco's temporary equilibrium is to be found in hard work balanced by the thrill of success.

Tagliatelle of Oysters and Caviar PAGE 28

Chicken Stock

1.5 kg/3 lb chicken wings
3.4l/6 pt water
2 carrots
1 stick of celery
2 whole leeks
3 onions
bouquet garni

•

1 Fill a deep saucepan with the cold water and add the chicken wings.
2 Bring the water to the boil and skim off any fat.
3 Wash and peel the vegetables and add to the stock with the bouquet garni.
4 Simmer for 3½ hours; pass through a sieve.

All the stocks included in this section can be frozen for up to 3 months without any problem.

Brown Veal Stock

900 g/2 lb veal meat (neck or shin of veal)
450 g/1 lb veal bones
1 pig's trotter, split
2 carrots
1 stick of celery
3 medium onions
3.4 l/6 pt water
bouquet garni (preferably fresh)

•

1 Brown the bones and the pig's trotter in a hot, greased roasting pan in the oven at 220°C/425°F/Gas Mark 7 – about 40 minutes.
2 Wash and peel the vegetables, then brown the vegetables and the meat in a deep saucepan.
3 Add the cold water and bring to the boil.
4 Add the roasted bones to the boiling water with bouquet garni and simmer for 5 hours.
5 Pass the stock through a sieve and leave to stand for 10 minutes. Skim the fat from the stock.
6 Boil the stock until it is reduced by half (you will end up with a *demi-glace*).

Vegetable Stock

1 onion
2 sticks of celery
1 leek
6 carrots
2 heads of garlic
5 white peppercorns
20 pink peppercorns
3 star anise
10 coriander seeds
3 slices of lemon
a sprig of chervil
a small bunch of tarragon
a small bunch of thyme
a small bunch of parsley
¼ bottle white wine

•

1 Chop all the vegetables into 5-mm/¼-in dice. Put them in a saucepan with the garlic, seasonings and herbs and just cover with water.
2 Bring to the boil and cook for 10 minutes.
3 Remove the pan from the heat and add the wine. Leave the mixture to infuse for about 1½ days in a cold place.
4 Sieve and use – freeze surplus for future use.

Velouté of Fish

10 shallots, finely chopped
25 g/1 oz butter
750 ml/1 ¼ pt Noilly Prat
750 ml/1 ¼ pt fish stock
750 ml/1 ¼ pt double cream

•

1 Cook the finely chopped shallots in the butter.
2 Add the Noilly Prat and cook until the mixture is reduced to a *glace* (a syrupy substance – you should be left with almost nothing).
3 Add the fish stock and reduce by half.
4 Add the cream and bring to the boil. Remove from the heat and leave for 10 minutes.
5 Sieve the mixture, and you have a velouté.

Potage of Oysters and Asparagus

SERVES 4

12 oysters
175 ml/6 fl oz oyster juice (taken from the shells of the oysters)
175 ml/6 fl oz vegetable stock (see page 27)
175 ml/6 fl oz velouté of fish (see page 27)
salt and pepper
lemon juice
12 asparagus spears
a little butter

•

1 Pour the oyster juice and vegetable stock into a saucepan with the oysters and poach for about 1 minute.
2 Add the velouté and bring the mixture back to the boil. Season and add lemon juice to taste.
3 Prepare the asparagus: peel and poach for 3 minutes in boiling salted water. Refresh the spears in cold water and drain.
4 When needed, reheat the asparagus in 2 tablespoons of water and the same amount of butter and cook until the water has evaporated and a glaze has formed over the top of the asparagus.
5 Arrange the oysters in soup bowls and pour over the soup.
6 Arrange the asparagus spears over the top.

Basic Pasta

500 g/18 oz plain flour
½ tsp salt
½ tsp olive oil
4 eggs
6 egg yolks

•

1 Put the flour, salt and olive oil in a mixer and process for a few seconds.
2 Add the eggs and yolks and mix until the pasta begins to come together.
3 Knead the pasta well on a flat surface until the mixture is even and smooth.

4 Cut into eight pieces, wrap each ball in clingfilm and allow to rest in the refrigerator for 20 minutes.
5 Preferably using a pasta machine, roll out the dough as finely as possible – this might take five or six rollings. Cut into very fine thin strips for tagliatelle, or into discs for ravioli or tortellini.

To make pasta successfully, do not try to make a smaller quantity than given here. You will need only half this quantity, however, to serve four people as an hors d'oeuvre. Any pasta left over can be kept in the freezer.

Tagliatelle of Oysters and Caviar

SERVES 4 AS AN HORS D'OEUVRE

pasta dough (see recipe above)
20 oysters No. 1 (opened and the rounded shells kept for serving)
olive oil
salt and pepper
a little lemon juice
25 g/1 oz butter

•

SAUCE
4 shallots, finely chopped
115 g/4 oz butter
70 ml/2 ½ fl oz champagne
70 ml/2 ½ fl oz vegetable stock or water
1 tbsp double cream
salt and pepper

•

GARNISH
225 g/8 oz cucumber (dark green in colour)
fresh seaweed or rock salt
2 tbsp caviar

•

1 Prepare the pasta and cut into fine strips as in the basic recipe. Cook in boiling salted water for 1 ½ minutes. Refresh in cold water, drain and toss in a little olive oil. Add salt, pepper and lemon juice to taste.

2 For the champagne butter sauce, cook the shallots gently in a little of the butter.

3 Add the champagne and cook to reduce until totally evaporated.

4 Add the vegetable stock or water and bring to the boil.

5 Add the cream and bring to the boil again.

6 Gradually whisk in the butter and then pass through a sieve. Season with salt and pepper.

7 Wash the oyster shells well, then place them in a small saucepan, cover with water and bring to the boil (to both clean and warm the oyster shells).

8 Poach the oysters in a separate pan, without boiling, for about 1½ minutes or until just firm to the touch.

9 In another pan, warm the pasta gently with a little butter and water, and season to taste.

10 Peel and seed the cucumber and cut into julienne strips about 4 cm/1½ in long. Cook in just enough water to cover and a little butter until the water has evaporated.

11 Dress each plate with seaweed or rock salt and place the oyster shells on top (five on each plate)

12 Cover the base of the shell with a little nest of tagliatelle (wind it round a fork to achieve the nest) and place an oyster on top. Garnish with cucumber strips.

13 Spoon the champagne butter sauce into each shell and top each oyster with a little caviar.

Ravioli of Crab and Ginger

SERVES 4 AS AN HORS D'OEUVRE

•

FILLING
pasta dough (see page 28)
100 g/3½ oz fillets of Dover sole
1 egg
salt and pepper
100 ml/3½ fl oz double cream
100 g/3½ oz crabmeat (white only)
10 fresh coriander leaves, blanched and chopped
10 g/¼ oz fresh ginger, finely chopped and blanched three times

SAUCE
150 ml/¼ pt vegetable stock
a little ginger root
4 segments of pink grapefruit
115 g/4 oz butter
salt and pepper
4 coriander leaves, coarsely chopped

•

1 Mix the fish, egg and seasoning for about 1 minute in a food processor.

2 Add the cream very slowly. Remove from the processor and pass through a sieve. Adjust seasoning.

3 Drain the crabmeat of any water, season and add to the mixture together with the blanched coriander and ginger. This is your filling for the ravioli.

4 Prepare the pasta and then roll out very finely (see basic recipe).

5 Cut it into discs – either a total of sixteen small discs 5 cm/2 in across or eight larger ones about 10 cm/4 in in diameter.

6 Place the mixture on half of the discs, and cover with the other discs. Cut round each ravioli with a fluted cutter.

7 Poach the ravioli in boiling salted water for 3 minutes.

8 To make the sauce, bring the vegetable stock to the boil with five small julienne strips of ginger.

9 Add the grapefruit segments and whisk the sauce until the segments have broken into small bits.

10 Gradually whisk in the butter, then adjust seasoning and add the coriander leaves.

11 Place two small ravioli or one larger one on each hot plate and dress with the sauce.

Ravioli of Lobster with a Sauce of Olive Oil PAGE 32

Noisettes of Lamb with a Tarragon Mousse PAGE 33

Tortellini or Ravioli of Lobster with a Sauce of Olive Oil

SERVES 4 AS AN HORS D'OEUVRE
pasta dough (see page 28)

•

100 g/3 ½ oz raw salmon
salt and pepper
½ egg white
120 ml/4 fl oz double cream
100 g/3 ½ oz cooked lobster tail
10 basil leaves, blanched and chopped
2 shallots, finely chopped
a little butter
½ tsp chopped truffle

•

SAUCE
1 clove of garlic
175 ml/6 fl oz olive oil
10 basil leaves
4 tomatoes
1 shallot, finely chopped
salt and pepper
a little lemon juice

•

GARNISH (optional)
a few slices of lobster tail
diced tomato

•

1 To make the filling, mix the salmon in a food processor with the seasoning for about 1 minute.
2 Add the egg white and mix for 15–20 seconds.
3 While the machine is still turning, add the cream very slowly.
4 Pass the mixture through a sieve and keep in the refrigerator.
5 Prepare the pasta and cut into discs using a round cutter as in the recipe for Ravioli of Crab and Ginger (see page 29).
6 Cut the cooked lobster tail into small dice and season before adding to the mousseline mixture with the chopped basil.
7 Cook the finely chopped shallots in a little butter until soft but not coloured and add to the mousseline with the chopped truffle.

8 To make tortellini, place a little mixture on each disc of pasta and then roll over to form a half moon shape. Press down with your fingers to seal the mixture inside. Use another cutter to even off the semi-circle. Wrap round your finger to make the crescent shape. Alternatively, simply make ravioli as in the previous recipe.
9 Poach the tortellini or ravioli in boiling salted water for 1 ½ or 3 minutes respectively.
10 For the sauce, peel the garlic clove, split it in half and heat it in a saucepan with the olive oil.
11 Blanch and finely chop the basil leaves and add to the oil.
12 Peel and de-seed the tomatoes, cut them into tiny dice and add to the oil.
13 In a separate pan, cook the finely chopped shallot gently in some olive oil without colouring, before adding this to the sauce.
14 Season with salt and pepper and a little lemon juice to taste.
15 Warm the pan gently on the side of the stove (not above direct heat) for about 15 minutes to let the mixture infuse.
16 Remove the clove of garlic and serve with the tortellini, garnished with slices of lobster tail and diced tomato, if liked.

Turbot with a Mustard Seed Sauce

SERVES 2
2 fillets of turbot weighing about 175 g/6 oz each
(keep the skin on the bottom)
2 shallots, sliced
a little butter
50 ml/2 fl oz dry white wine
100 ml/3 ½ fl oz fish stock
salt and pepper
300 ml/ ½ pt velouté of fish (see page 27)
1 tsp grainy mustard (Moutarde de Meaux)
1 tbsp chopped chives
a little lemon juice (optional)

1 Cook the sliced shallots in a knob of butter.

2 Deglaze the pan with wine and boil until it has evaporated. Add the fish stock and bring to the boil.

3 Place the seasoned fillets, skin side up, in the stock and put the butter paper over the fish.

4 Cook the fish in the oven at 180°C/350°F/Gas Mark 4 for about 4–5 minutes.

5 Bring the velouté to the boil in a saucepan.

6 Remove from the stove and whisk in a knob of butter, the mustard and the chopped chives. Season to taste – if necessary add a dash of lemon juice. Keep the sauce warm.

7 Take the fish out of the cooking stock and dry it on kitchen paper.

8 Place the fillets skin side upwards and coat them with the sauce.

This is best served with fresh pasta.

Sea Bass with Fresh Basil

SERVES 4

1.25 kg/2 ½ lb sea bass
200 g/7 oz scallops
a pinch of cayenne pepper
salt
250 ml/9 fl oz double cream
a dash of lemon juice
8 basil leaves, blanched (to remove bitterness)
10 g/¼ oz truffle, cut into very tiny particles
pepper

•

SAUCE
1 carrot
1 leek
1 stick of celery
400 ml/14 fl oz vegetable stock
4 scallops
1 basil leaf
50 g/2 oz butter
salt and pepper
a dash of lemon juice

1 Separate the sea bass into two fillets and then cut these in half (keep the skin on the bottom).

2 Liquidize the scallops for 1 minute, add a pinch of cayenne pepper and salt and the cream, and liquidize again.

3 Pass the mixture through a sieve, adjust seasoning and add the lemon juice if it is needed.

4 Add half the blanched, chopped basil and the particles of truffle.

5 Season the fish with salt and pepper. Slit each of the four fillets and stuff with the mousse. Wrap in clingfilm with a piece of basil leaf in each parcel.

6 Steam the fish for about 5 minutes.

7 For the sauce, cut the carrot, leek and celery into julienne strips and blanch in boiling salted water. Refresh in cold water.

8 Bring the vegetable stock to the boil and add the vegetables and the scallops, cut into cubes.

9 Cut the basil into *chiffonades* (thin strips) and add to the sauce with the butter. Cook gently until the sauce is velvety. Season to taste and add a dash of lemon juice, if necessary.

10 To serve, divide the sauce between the four plates and place the sea bass fillets on top, skin side upwards. Season to taste.

Noisettes of Lamb with a Tarragon Mousse

SERVES 4

2 racks of lamb from a best end weighing
2.75 kg/5–6 lb
enough crépinette (caul or web of fat) to wrap 8 noisettes

•

TARRAGON MOUSSE
200 g/7 oz chicken breasts
a pinch of mace
salt
1 egg
225 ml/8 fl oz double cream
1 tbsp chopped tarragon

Roast Guinea Fowl with a Sauce of Madeira

SAUCE

lamb bones from the best end, chopped
a mirepoix of ½ onion, 2 medium carrots and
¼ stick of celery
a little butter
1 large clove of garlic, split
25 ml/1 fl oz brandy
100 ml/3 ½ fl oz Madeira
200 ml/7 fl oz dry white wine
veal stock (two-thirds of the volume needed)
chicken stock (one-third of the volume needed)
a sprig of thyme
a sprig of tarragon
¹⁄₁₀ bay leaf
5 white peppercorns
4 medium tomatoes, de-seeded and diced
1 chicken leg (optional)
4 tarragon leaves, chopped
salt and pepper

•

1 Cut each rack into four pieces – so you have eight double cutlets in all. Remove one bone from each double cutlet and scrape the remaining bone clean.

2 For the sauce, roast the lamb bones in the oven at 220°C/425°F/Gas Mark 7 for 30 minutes until brown but not too dark.

3 In a separate pan, sweat the *mirepoix* of onion, carrot and celery in a knob of butter with the split garlic. Allow to caramelize slowly.

4 Add the roasted bones to the pan containing the vegetables and deglaze with the brandy. Add the Madeira and bring the mixture to the boil. Add the white wine and reduce completely.

5 Cover the bones with two-thirds veal stock to one-third chicken stock – make sure the bones are covered. Add the sprigs of thyme and tarragon, bay leaf, peppercorns, tomatoes (reserving a few for garnish) and chicken leg, if used. Bring to the boil and simmer for 35 minutes.

6 Open up the *crépinette* – you need eight pieces.

7 To make the tarragon mousse, mix the chicken with the mace and salt to taste for 1 minute in a processor. Add the egg and mix for another minute. Add the cream and mix for a further minute. Adjust seasoning. Pass through a sieve and add the chopped tarragon.

8 Put some tarragon mousse on each piece of *crépinette* and place a cutlet on top and then more mousse on top of this. Cover each cutlet with the *crépinette* to form a parcel.

9 Brown the *crépinette* parcels carefully in a frying pan (take care they don't split). Take out of the pan.

10 When the stock is ready, pass it through a fine sieve and return to the pan. Boil until reduced by one-third.

11 Put a layer of butter paper in a roasting tray, butter side upwards, and place the lamb noisettes on top with the best sides uppermost. Put them in the oven at 220°C/425°F/Gas Mark 7 for about 8 minutes; the lamb should be pink.

12 Add the chopped tarragon leaves to the sauce and boil for 15 seconds. Add the reserved diced tomatoes and season.

13 Pour some of the sauce onto each plate and place two noisettes on top.

Roast Guinea Fowl with a Sauce of Madeira

SERVES 2

1 guinea fowl weighing 1.25 kg/2 ½ lb
25 ml/1 fl oz oil
a little butter
4 shallots, chopped
85 g/3 oz button mushrooms
½ clove of garlic
a sprig of thyme
1 dried morel
a dash of cognac
100 ml/3 ½ fl oz Madeira
chicken stock (enough to cover bones)
1 tbsp double cream
salt and pepper
a dash of lemon juice

GARNISH
10 whites of baby leeks
10 medium girolles
10 button onions
85 g/3 oz butter
1 tbsp chicken stock
a dash of lemon juice

•

1 To prepare the guinea fowl, chop off the wings and feet (keep these for the sauce) and remove the wishbone, then truss.

2 Heat some of the oil in a roasting pan and brown the guinea fowl on all sides. Cover with buttered foil and cook in the oven at 220°C/425°F/Gas Mark 7 for about 25 minutes.

3 For the sauce, chop the wings and meat scraps and brown in a saucepan with the remaining oil.

4 Add the shallots, button mushrooms and garlic and sweat them together until caramelized.

5 Add the thyme and morel, and deglaze the pan with a dash of cognac. Cook until reduced almost completely.

6 Add the Madeira and reduce entirely.

7 Cover the bones with chicken stock and cook slowly for about 20 minutes. Sieve.

8 Bring the stock to the boil, whisk in the cream and a knob of butter. Season to taste and add the lemon juice if it needs it.

9 For the garnish, blanch the leeks in boiling salted water until tender. Refresh in cold water and then cook again with a knob of butter and the chicken stock until the stock has evaporated.

10 Cook the *girolles* in a little butter and a dash of lemon juice. Adjust seasoning. Cook the button onions in 25 g/1 oz of butter until golden brown.

11 To serve, remove the legs from the bird and separate the thigh from the drumstick. Clean the end of each drumstick and remove the bone from the thigh. Season. Remove the breasts in one piece from the bone.

12 Put a thigh in the middle of a serving plate and place a drumstick next to it. Carve the breast and place on top of the thigh and drumstick. Season.

13 Pour the sauce around the guinea fowl. Arrange the vegetable garnish round it.

Tagliatelle of Vegetables

SERVES 1
1 large leek
1 large courgette
1 large carrot
100 ml/3 ½ fl oz water
100 g/3 ½ oz butter
salt and pepper

•

1 Wash all the vegetables.

2 Remove the dark green leaves from the leek and cut down the middle lengthways into about 15-cm/6-in lengths that are 5 mm/¼ in wide and 1 cm/½ in thick.

3 Cut the courgette lengthways and remove the seeds and ends. Cut in the same way as for the leek.

4 Cut the carrot in the same way.

5 Blanch the carrot in boiling salted water and refresh in cold water.

6 Blanch the leek in boiling salted water and then refresh in cold water.

7 Bring the water and butter to the boil in a separate pan. Add the carrot and cook briefly until just pliable, then put in the leek. When the carrot is almost cooked but still crisper than *al dente*, add the courgette to warm through. Drain and season with salt and pepper. (Always use the carrot as the gauge of your cooking times for the other vegetables.)

8 To serve, wrap the vegetables round a fork to form a circular shape.

This goes very well with lamb.

Braised Lettuce

SERVES 4

1 round lettuce (discard the outer leaves)
100 ml/3 ½ fl oz chicken stock
25 ml/1 fl oz veal stock
10 g/ ¼ oz butter
salt and pepper

•

1 Cut the lettuce into four (leaving the stalk on but cleaning up the bottom of the stalk – don't cut it off!).

2 Blanch the lettuce in boiling salted water for 15 seconds. Refresh in cold water. Drain and allow to dry.

3 Put the chicken and veal stock in a small pan and bring to the boil. Add the lettuce.

4 Place in the oven at 220°C/425°F/Gas Mark 7 for about 5 minutes or until tender.

5 Remove the pan from the oven and boil rapidly on top of the stove until the liquid has been reduced by half. Add the butter and season.

Serve the lettuce with meat such as quail, foie gras or rabbit.

Nougat Glace with a Coulis of Raspberries

This is best made the day before you need it.

•

SERVES 8

6 egg whites
450 g/1 lb caster sugar
100 g/3 ½ oz roasted hazelnuts, husks removed
200 g/7 oz sugar lumps
325 ml/11 fl oz double cream, whipped
300 g/11 oz raspberries
lemon juice to taste

•

1 Beat the egg whites with 250 g/9 oz of sugar until it forms a stiff meringue.

2 To make the praline, cook the hazelnuts and

sugar lumps until you have a caramel. Let it cool on an oiled surface or greaseproof paper.

3 Mix the whipped cream into the meringue.

4 Smash the praline into small pieces and add to the mixture.

5 Line a loaf tin with clingfilm and pour in the mixture. Freeze it for about 12 hours.

6 For the sauce, liquidize the remaining sugar and raspberries and pass through a sieve. Add lemon juice to taste if needed.

7 Serve a slice of the *glace* on a bed of the sauce.

Honey Ice Cream with an Orange Sauce

SERVES 8

6 egg yolks
50 g/2 oz caster sugar
500 ml/18 fl oz milk
150 g/5 oz clear honey
85 ml/3 fl oz double cream

•

SAUCE

150 ml/ ¼ pt Crème Anglaise (see page 84)
1 tbsp double cream
1 tbsp fresh orange juice

•

1 Whisk together the egg yolks and the sugar.

2 Boil the milk in a saucepan and pour over the egg yolk and sugar mixture.

3 Pour the hot mixture back into the pan and cook, stirring continuously, until the mixture has thickened to a custard. Pass through a sieve into a cold bowl.

4 Whisk in the honey and then, while still hot, the double cream.

5 Put in an ice cream maker and freeze.

6 Serve this with an orange sauce, made by mixing the *crème anglaise* with a tablespoon each of double cream and fresh orange juice.

Gunn Eriksen

I had arranged to meet the Altnaharrie Ferry at the jetty in Ullapool at 4.45 p.m. on the Monday before Easter. As it was nearly five o'clock, this impatient Londoner asked the man painting the underbelly of the *Summer Queen* cruiser whether the ferry had been over recently. 'Everything is late in Ullapool – you'll soon get used to that,' he advised me as I stamped my feet in the biting cold. Keeping that philosophy in mind, imagine setting up a restaurant producing high-quality food when everything has to arrive by boat.

In 1980 that was the challenge facing Gunn Eriksen when she and Fred, quite by accident, took over the running of the Altnaharrie Inn in Ullapool. It is possible to reach Altnaharrie by road – provided, that is, you have a four-wheel drive vehicle and a lot of nerve to make it down the 2½-mile stone track. Inverness, the nearest town of any size, is a good 1½ hours' drive away. Yet with all these difficulties, in a surprisingly short time Gunn and Fred have built up a reputation across the country for 'real food' – food that doesn't follow any fashion, however the guides may try to label it. 'Modern British cooking' is the latest stamp from *The Good Food Guide* – much to Gunn's suprise: 'What on earth does it mean? I'm not deliberately trying to do anything; I'm just cooking in the way I know.' And yet, with an equivalent rating to the Dorchester Hotel, the Altnaharrie Inn is in the Top Ten League of restaurants in the country. All of which made Gunn want to run a mile: 'I felt such an imposter – after all, I never wanted to cook professionally.'

When Gunn met Fred, he was a vet with a growing interest in yacht chartering and, after an art school training in Norway, Gunn was in Inverness to learn more about pottery and tapestrywork. On her second day in Scotland, Gunn met Fred and that, as they say, was that. But neither of them expected to run the Altnaharrie Inn. Although his second wife had taken paying guests at the inn, it was primarily a home and a base from which Fred hoped to expand his boat business. After his wife died, when Fred had met Gunn, they appointed managers for the season. Two weeks before the first full house of ten guests were due, they backed out and Fred and Gunn had to go it alone.

Gunn simply had to rely on what she had learned as a child from her mother at home in Grimstadt, between Stavanger and Oslo. Now as her confidence grows so do her ideas: 'I can only cook well when I'm very busy and when I'm very hungry – that's when the ideas come.' And Gunn's inspiration for her dishes rarely comes from what she reads but from what she sees around her. A stone on the shore of the Loch with some seaweed peeping out from underneath it prompted a light pastry case with an asparagus mousse trapped beneath it. Dishes have to have contrasting textures, shapes and colours if they are to delight Gunn. She admits that her art school background influences her approach and, just as she considers colour, depth and texture in a tapestrywork study, so she brings the same influences to bear on food. Gunn remembers the message from her art teacher: yes, respect the works of the old masters and learn your techniques from them but never, never copy. Gunn vows she would actually do a U-turn if she found herself doing it.

Gunn is actually very lucky to be far enough away from 'foodie' pressures to enjoy the freedom to do what she wants, in spite of the constraints on food supplies. Fish is plentiful and good, but it has taken time to convince the smoked haddock suppliers of Lochinver not to stain their haddock bright yellow, and time too to tell the fishermen about wolf-fish. Wolf-fish is a popular fish in Norway – feeding as it does on shellfish, its flesh has a beautiful flavour. 'Do always examine the stomach of a fish – that way you learn a lot about its composition and its flavour. The way a fish is killed is important too. Somehow chemicals must be emitted when a fish panics as it's caught, and, yes, this does affect the flavour.' Actually, Gunn doesn't like serving salmon in Scotland – except as a garnish or perhaps as *gravadlax* for lunch – because she believes people touring Scotland must be heartily sick of salmon. She cares a great deal about guests' preferences and keeps diaries which help her check what people have eaten on previous visits. The challenge is to always give people new dishes, which can be difficult when they stay for a fortnight. This is how recipes like Hawthorn and Cucumber Soup and Nettle and Brie Soup crept into the menu. Gunn was in the garden picking flowers for the tables and wondering how on earth she was going to produce something different for the long-staying guest. She nibbled a bit of young hawthorn leaf on her way past and she imagined its nutty taste with cucumber, and so a new soup was born.

Gunn's love of using things wild is part of her philosophy of the balance of life – of fitting into her surroundings. 'Only an obsessive idiot would spend two hours with her feet in cold water with midges attacking every part of her body picking enough wild raspberries for tonight's pudding.' Gunn often has to stop guests weeding the front garden at Altnaharrie because unwittingly they are destroying essential ingredients, like ground elder, bittercress or nettles.

Guests here are obviously disarmed by this pretty, sensitive, fastidious young woman who cares so much about their welfare. Gunn actually takes a bath in every bathroom to get a guest's eye view of the ceiling or the underside of the windowsill, or the walls. Not only that but she tests all the beds for comfort during the season, by sleeping in them as they become vacant.

Without Gunn, Altnaharrie would collapse. Fred knows that. Although he waits at table and deals with all the problems that crop up at Altnaharrie, without Gunn the place couldn't function. Her stamp is clearly on everything and, although she has a handful of young, loyal staff, she is the one to check the flowers are right, the bedrooms are utterly clean and the kitchen and dining room are up to her incredibly high standards. But the challenge of such hard work from Easter to October provides the adrenalin to produce the stamina Gunn needs, and she gets enormous satisfaction hearing the sounds of happy people eating in her dining room as she cooks their dinner. Two Americans coming back on the ferry about to savour their second Altnaharrie dinner were as excited as small children. They took me through last night's meal – crab soup, asparagus mousse in a case of pastry, pigeon in its own juices, a salad, and then, joy of joys, not one but three puddings: a lemon tart, a Norwegian cream trifle, and a gooey hot chocolate cake. They could hardly contain themselves.

Gunn is a reluctant star. She doesn't have much confidence in herself, is a terrible self-critic, and frankly can't understand why people are fêting her the way they are. Her name in Norwegian means 'fight' – and that is just what she has done. Gunn has fought local complacency, laziness, suppliers who believed anything would do, the sheer geographical complexities of Altnaharrie, and she has achieved in that little drover's inn an atmosphere that is quite unique, utterly charming, and food that defies categories save one – that it is very, very good.

Marrow and Coriander Soup

SERVES 4–6

750 g/1 ¾ lb marrow
2 medium potatoes
½ onion
1 l/1 ¾ pt water
100 g/3 ½ oz Brie cheese
a small handful of coriander leaves
a few sprigs of parsley
salt and pepper
freshly ground nutmeg
lemon juice to taste

•

GARNISH
a little double cream
coriander leaves and flowers

•

1 Chop the marrow, potatoes and onion, and boil in the water until tender.
2 Liquidize the vegetables together with the Brie and herbs, then put through a coarse sieve.
3 Season with salt and pepper and freshly ground nutmeg and a little lemon juice to taste.
4 Serve the soup with a freestyle pattern of cream, a fresh coriander leaf and maybe a few flowers for garnish.

Hawthorn and Cucumber Soup

SERVES 4–6

500 g/18 oz young hawthorn leaves
1 large cucumber
1 l/1 ¾ pt strong pigeon stock
½ onion
1 potato
salt and pepper
nutmeg
lemon juice
double cream
hawthorn leaves and flowers for garnish

1 Boil the pigeon stock with the chopped onion and potato.
2 Add the freshly picked hawthorn leaves and simmer for 2–3 minutes.
3 Liquidize the mixture together with the raw cucumber. Pass through a sieve and season with salt, pepper and nutmeg.
4 Warm the mixture up but make sure it doesn't boil – the cucumber must remain raw.
5 Just before serving add lemon juice and cream to taste.
6 To garnish, float young hawthorn leaves and flowers on top of each serving.

Prawns in Port

SERVES 4 AS AN HORS D'OEUVRE

16 large langoustines (Dublin Bay prawns)
70 g/2 ½ oz butter
50 ml/2 fl oz Remy Martin (cognac)
3 shallots
150 ml/ ¼ pt port
250 ml/9 fl oz double cream
1 tsp Dijon mustard
2 egg yolks
salt and freshly crushed pepper
chopped parsley mixed with dill for garnish

•

1 Sauté the whole langoustines with the butter in a large, heavy iron pan.
2 Flambé with the cognac.
3 Add the chopped shallots, cook until soft, then add the port. Turn the langoustines until cooked.
4 In a separate bowl, mix the cream, mustard and egg yolks and then add to the pan; keep warm but do not boil. Taste and adjust seasoning.
5 Pour some sauce onto a warm plate, add the langoustines and then top again with sauce. Garnish with chopped parsley and dill.

Lamb Sweetbreads with a Wild Sorrel and Mustard Sauce

SERVES 4 AS AN HORS D'OEUVRE

350 g/12 oz lamb sweetbreads (make sure you ask for thymus)
25 g/1 oz butter
wild sorrel leaves for garnish

•

PASTRY

150 g/5 oz plain flour
2 ½ tbsp cold water
1 very small egg (even half an egg if large)
1 small tsp sunflower oil
100 g/3 ½ oz butter

•

SAUCE

3 shallots, finely chopped
50 g/2 oz butter
200 ml/7 fl oz double cream
1 large tbsp coarse-grain mustard
1 large tbsp rowan jelly
a little lemon juice (optional)
a large handful of wild sorrel leaves
salt and coarsely ground pepper

•

1 Put the sweetbreads to soak in cold water while you prepare the strudel pastry.

2 Mix the flour, water and egg in a mixer, then cover the dough with a little sunflower oil (this prevents a skin forming and adds flavour) and leave to rest for 30 minutes.

3 Roll out the dough onto a floured cloth until it is paper thin.

4 Melt the butter, brush half the dough with it and fold the other half over it. Cut the dough into pieces 7.5 × 12.5 cm/3 × 5 in.

5 Drape the dough halfway round an upturned ramekin, making a cave-like shape. Where the dough gathers at the top use a string of dough to bind it together. Brush with butter and cook in the oven at 220°C/425°F/Gas Mark 7 for 10 minutes until golden and crisp. Remove the ramekins.

6 Remove all the sinews and blood from the sweetbreads, take out of the water and dry on kitchen towel.

7 To make the sauce, sauté the shallots gently in the butter. Add the cream, mustard, rowan jelly and a little lemon juice to taste if it is needed.

8 Liquidize half the sorrel and add it to the sauce. Chop the rest of the sorrel into thin strips and add to the sauce. Taste and adjust seasoning.

9 Heat a frying pan, add the butter and seal the sweetbreads, then toss until lightly cooked. Drain the sweetbreads and add to the sauce.

10 Arrange a little of the sweetbreads and sauce on each warmed plate, place a freshly-baked cave of pastry on top of the sweetbreads and a cluster of sorrel leaves at the cave opening. Serve at once.

Wolf-Fish with a Salmon Cream

Served on a Sauce of Bittercress and Champagne

•

SERVES 4

2.75 kg/6 lb wolf-fish or 1 medium turbot
150 g/5 oz raw salmon
100 ml/3 ½ fl oz double cream
lemon juice to taste
225 ml/8 fl oz Chablis
coarse sea salt and freshly ground pepper

•

BITTERCRESS SAUCE

½ Spanish onion
50 g/2 oz butter
225 ml/8 fl oz milk
a good handful of bittercress (you should find this in your lawn – it has a similar flavour to watercress but milder)
225 ml/8 fl oz champagne
100 ml/3 ½ fl oz double cream

•

1 Fillet the fish so that you have four good fillets. Twist each fillet into a circle, secure with a cocktail stick and set aside.

2 Chop up the raw salmon and mix with the

double cream and a little lemon juice. Liquidize until the mixture is smooth. Taste to check flavour, and put the mixture in a piping bag.

3 To make the bittercress sauce, sweat the chopped onion in the butter in a saucepan until the onion is just soft. Add the milk and simmer for a few minutes. Put this mixture in the liquidizer with the washed bittercress, and process.

4 Put the Chablis in a baking dish and top up with hot water so that the liquid is 2.5 cm/1 in deep. Add coarse salt and pepper. Place the fillets in the dish and cook in the oven, covered with foil, at 190°C/375°F/Gas Mark 5 for 5–10 minutes (but always check that the fish is still firm – err towards undercooked fish not overcooked).

5 Sieve the liquidized sauce, return it to the pan and add the champagne and cream. Heat but do not allow to boil – taste and adjust seasoning.

6 Pour some bittercress sauce onto each plate. Place the fish on the sauce and pipe the raw salmon into the inner circle.

7 Garnish with fresh bittercress and a flower of marinaded salmon.

Lobster Served Slightly Warm with Two Sauces

SERVES 4
2 lobsters, each weighing 450–675 g/1–1 ½ lb
ground elder and chervil for garnish
•
COLD RED LOBSTER SAUCE
dark meat and roes of lobster
100 ml/3 ½ fl oz soured cream
salt and pepper
lemon juice
•
WARM VEGETABLE SAUCE
50 g/2 oz butter
6–8 dill seeds
6–8 coriander seeds
1 fennel
½ onion

2 carrots
200 ml/7 fl oz Mâcon Villages Clessé white wine
2 egg yolks
100 ml/3 ½ fl oz double cream
salt and pepper
•

1 Boil the lobsters in salted water for 3–5 minutes, then leave them to go cold in their cooking water. Drain.

2 Remove the claws in one piece and save the dark meat from the head and roes for the cold sauce. Set aside the tails.

3 Mix the dark meat and roes in a liquidizer with the soured cream. Season and add lemon juice to taste, pass through a sieve and set aside.

4 To make the warm vegetable sauce, put the butter in a thick-bottomed saucepan and add the dill and coriander seeds first, to ensure their flavour is fully emitted.

5 Put the chopped fennel, chopped onion and carrots in the pan. Cook gently until *al dente*.

6 Pour the contents of the pan into the liquidizer and give a short spin to cut the vegetables without producing a mush. Strain the liquid through a sieve and throw the vegetables away.

7 Put the juice from the vegetables in the pan and add the wine and the lobster heads for flavour. Cook to reduce the liquid a little.

8 Mix the egg yolks with the double cream, and add to the sauce to thicken. Warm gently, pass the sauce through a sieve and season with salt and pepper.

9 Pour some warm sauce onto the plate and in the centre put a little of the cold pink sauce. Slice the lobster tails across into medallions and place in a line on one side with the whole claw facing upwards.

10 Garnish with ground elder and chervil.

Wolf-Fish with a Salmon Cream PAGE 41

Chunky Fish Soup Served with Moules Marinières

SERVES 4–6

750 g/1 ¾ lb fish (comprising salmon, monkfish, wolf-fish, lemon sole, brill and torsk – or whatever firm fresh fish is available)
bones from the white fish
½ onion
50–100 g/2–3 ½ oz butter
½ tsp turmeric
½ tsp paprika
½ tsp dill seeds
3–4 strands of saffron
4 tomatoes
a sprig of rosemary
2 bay leaves
½ bottle dry white burgundy wine
250 ml/9 fl oz double cream
1 spring onion, chopped
1 large tbsp chopped dill
1 large tbsp chopped flat parsley
1 large tbsp chopped fennel

•

GARNISH
2 prawns per person
3 spinies (squat lobsters) per person
1 tbsp double cream
sprigs of parsley and dill or fronds of fennel

•

MOULES MARINIÈRES
at least 10–15 mussels per person
½ onion
½ clove of garlic
a pinch of paprika
a pinch of cayenne pepper
a pinch of chilli powder
pepper
2 tbsp chopped parsley
½ bottle dry white burgundy wine

•

1 Fillet the fish, and put the bones from the white fish in a large saucepan with enough water to cover to make a stock. Simmer for about 1 hour.

When ready, strain the liquor – you need 1 litre/1 ¾ pt of fish stock.

2 Put the chopped onion in a saucepan with the butter, turmeric, paprika, dill seeds and saffron.

3 Peel the tomatoes and add to the pan; push them down using a potato masher.

4 Add the rosemary, bay leaves and the fish stock. Cook for 1 hour.

5 Add the wine and cream, and then the spring onion, dill, parsley and fennel. Simmer for about 10 minutes.

6 Then prepare the Moules Marinières: put the mussels in a large saucepan with the onion, garlic, paprika, cayenne, chilli, pepper and parsley. Add the white wine – but if you are using lemon sole in the main recipe, reserve 50 ml/2 fl oz – and poach for a few minutes until the mussels open.

7 Place all the fish except the lemon sole in the pot of soup to poach, starting with the most resilient, such as monkfish. Do not allow the liquid to boil but simply warm the fish – the texture should remain firm.

8 If using lemon sole, form each fillet into a little roll and secure with a cocktail stick. Poach in a separate pan in two-thirds water and one-third wine reserved from the mussels (you need just enough liquid to cover the bottom of the pan) to ensure that the rolls of fish are not overcooked and do not flake. Drain and add the lemon sole to the soup.

9 To serve, pour the soup into bowls, sharing out the fish pieces, and garnish with the steamed prawns and spinies (if available), a swirl of cream and the dill or fennel. Put the mussels in a communal bowl and garnish with parsley.

Mousseline of Scallops Inlaid with Crab

Served under a Shell of Pastry with a Sauce of Juices of Ham

•

SERVES 4

8 large scallops
2 good crabs (use the crabmeat from the 4 large claws and legs)
200 ml/7 fl oz soured cream
100 ml/3 ½ fl oz double cream
salt and pepper
a pinch of nutmeg
juice of ½ lemon
4 slices of truffle
150 g/5 oz pastry (see Lamb Sweetbreads recipe on page 41)
sprigs of coriander for garnish

•

SAUCE

1.5–1.75 kg/3–4 lb ham bones or 450 g/1 lb joint of smoked pork loin
coarse-grain mustard
a dash of red wine (a good burgundy)
1 dessertsp double cream
salt and pepper

•

1 To make the sauce, coat the ham bones or joint of pork loin with a little mustard and roast in the oven at 220°C/425°F/Gas Mark 7 for 30–40 minutes.

2 Put the bones or the joint in a saucepan, cover with water and cook until the liquid is quite reduced. Drain the juices from the bones or meat.

3 Add a dash of red wine and the cream to the stock. Cook until reduced – the resulting sauce should be only 8–10 tablespoons of liquid. Taste and adjust seasoning – it should taste of a hint of ham and a vague flavour of wine, but neither should be overpowering. Keep the sauce warm.

4 Prepare the mousseline: clean the scallops, setting aside 4 corals, 4 thin slices of scallop cut crossways, and the ends of the 4 large crab claws for garnish.

5 Liquidize the remaining scallop meat with the soured cream.

6 Sieve this mixture and add the double cream, salt, pepper and nutmeg and the lemon juice if needed. The mixture should be very light.

7 Butter four little ramekins or dariole moulds and place a layer of scallop mixture in them, then a little crabmeat, and keep layering. The last layer should be the scallop mixture, but let the crabmeat layer preceding it contain a little of the red coral from the crab.

8 Make the strudel pastry: follow instructions in the Lamb Sweetbreads recipe, but totally cover the mould, twirling the top of the mould into a rose.

9 Put the pastry mould in the top of the oven at 220°C/425°F/Gas Mark 7 for about 4 minutes before adding the scallop moulds.

10 Place the scallop moulds over hot water in a bain-marie and cook at the bottom of the oven for 5–10 minutes (at the same time as the pastry is cooking at the top). Do check timing – Agas, on which I cook, are very different from gas and electric ovens!

11 Warm the slices of truffle in the sauce and reserve for garnishing.

12 Pour some sauce on each plate and add the mousseline of scallop. Decorate the mousseline with a small sprig of coriander.

13 Place the shell of pastry over the mousseline. Arrange the slice of scallop coming from the shell as if spilling from underneath, top with the piece of crab claw and place the coral of scallop by the side.

14 Place a larger sprig of coriander and a slice of truffle on the other side.

This dish thrives on a good red burgundy.

Chunky Fish Soup Served with Moules Marinières PAGE *44*

Marinated Bonito

Tuna or mackerel will do, but this fish is delicious. It is very important to use fresh fish for this and not frozen.

•

SERVES 4
1 kg/2 ¼ lb fillets of bonito
50 g/2 oz sugar
50 g/2 oz salt
freshly ground black pepper
a pinch of dill seeds
½ clove of garlic, crushed to yield juice
a handful of chopped flat parsley
a handful of chopped coriander leaves

•

GARNISH
fresh coriander leaves and flat parsley
soured cream
a little caviar

•

1 Mix together the sugar, salt, pepper and dill seeds. Use to cover the fish fillets which should retain the bottom skin.
2 Sprinkle on the garlic juice.
3 Make a bed of the parsley and coriander leaves in the bottom of the dish. Place half the fillets of bonito on top.
4 Place another layer of parsley and coriander, and on top another layer of fish.
5 Place a weight on top of this and leave in the refrigerator, covered, for 2 days. Turn every 12 hours. Remove from the marinade.
6 Serve in thin slices cut at an angle, as you would smoked salmon. (It will be easier to slice the fish if you put it in the freezer to firm up the flesh for a short while.)
7 Using some bonito to curl underneath to give it height, make a fan of sliced bonito. On one side of the fan, place a sprig of coriander and parsley and on the other side a blob of soured cream topped with a little caviar.

Medallions of Hare

Served in a Sauce of its Own Juices with Grapes, Juniper and Dill

The combination of dill and game is quite unusual and very delicious. I always use mountain hare as this has a much lovelier flavour than brown hare and is much less gamey.

•

SERVES 4
2 hares (allow a saddle between two people)
2 small leeks
85 g/3 oz butter
enough water or stock to cover
a handful of grapes
225 ml/8 fl oz red wine
12 juniper berries
1 tbsp dill
extra butter for frying
3 tbsp Armagnac
salt and pepper

•

GARNISH
12 seedless green grapes
3 tbsp double cream
20–28 sprigs of dill

•

1 Fillet the saddle from the hares. Cut the meat into 2.5-cm/1-in medallions (5–7 per person).
2 Roast the bones together with the leeks and 85 g/3 oz butter in the oven at 220°C/425°F/Gas Mark 7 for 30–40 minutes. When quite brown, put in a large saucepan and cover with water or stock. Boil for several hours with a handful of grapes. Skim and strain and transfer to a smaller saucepan.
3 Continue boiling until quite reduced. Add the red wine, juniper berries and dill, and boil again until reduced – you should be left with about 120 ml/4 fl oz. Taste frequently.
4 Heat the extra knob of butter in a frying pan. When very hot, add the medallions of hare and fry for a few seconds on both sides.

5 Add the Armagnac and flambé. Remove the meat and add the juices to the sauce. Taste and adjust seasonings.

6 Put a little sauce on each plate and arrange the medallions in a circle.

7 Decorate with seedless green grapes and a swirl of cream and top each slice with a sprig of dill.

Breast of Duck with Port and a Touch of Orange

SERVES 4

2 × 2.25-kg/5-lb free-range ducklings (including livers)
8 spring onions (left whole)
100 ml/3 ½ fl oz red wine
coarsely ground black pepper
juice and zest of 1 orange
1 tsp lemon juice
sprigs of tarragon
salt
15 g/ ½ oz butter
sprigs of watercress

•

1 Remove all the meat, fat and skin from the ducklings, keeping the breasts in their shape. Set all this aside. The legs are not needed for this recipe, but can be used in a host of other dishes.

2 Roast the carcasses with the spring onions without any extra fat in the oven at 220°C/425°F/Gas Mark 7 until brown and crisp.

3 Place the bones in a large saucepan, cover with water and boil for a few hours until the bones fall apart. Strain and leave the mixture to cool. Skim all the fat from the stock.

4 Bring the stock to the boil, add the red wine and reduce until about 500 ml/18 fl oz of liquid remains. Add some pepper, the orange juice, lemon juice and a sprig of tarragon. Keep boiling and tasting – the orange flavour should only be faint. The final volume of sauce should be between 8 and 10 tablespoons.

5 Take the breasts and remove all the sinews, but retain the skin on each breast. Cut all surplus skin into long thin strips, sprinkle with salt and put in a hot frying pan. Don't use any extra fat, but allow the skins to cook until crisp and golden. Put the skins on kitchen paper to remove all traces of fat. Retain for use in the Plum and Endive Salad (see page 51).

6 Take the livers and cut them into long thin strips; wash well and dry.

7 Rub the flesh of the breasts with a little salt and pepper, then seal them in a hot pan. Remove and cook under the grill to your liking (they should really be pink in the middle).

8 Remove the skin from the cooked breasts and slice the meat into strips.

9 Toss the liver strips in the hot butter.

10 Arrange the breasts in a fan shape on top of some of the sauce and decorate with the livers, sprigs of tarragon, watercress and the zest of the orange.

Serve this dish with the Plum and Endive Salad (see page 51) and sugar-glazed potatoes–boil very tiny new potatoes and then toss them in 100 g/3 ½ oz of glazing sugar (sugar that has been mixed with 1 tablespoon of water and melted and browned), thinning out with more water if necessary.

Mousseline of Scallops Inlaid with Crab PAGE 45

Broccoli and Mushrooms in Soured Cream and Coriander Sauce

Served with Homemade Tagliatelle

•

SERVES 4

•

TAGLIATELLE
200 g/7 oz plain flour
2 eggs
a little olive oil
salt

•

SAUCE
250 ml/9 fl oz soured cream
2 egg yolks
a pinch of freshly ground coriander seeds
coarsley ground black pepper
lemon juice to taste

•

VEGETABLES
50 g/2 oz butter
½ clove of garlic
100 g/3 ½ oz mushrooms (very firm and white)
250 g/9 oz broccoli tips (florets)

•

GARNISH
freshly chopped coriander leaves

•

1 Mix together the ingredients for the pasta and leave to rest for about 30 minutes.
2 Roll the dough through a pasta machine or roll out with a rolling pin and cut into strips.
3 To make the sauce, mix the soured cream, egg yolks, coriander, pepper and lemon juice together and warm gently. Do not allow to boil.
4 Prepare the vegetables: melt the butter in a frying pan, add the crushed garlic, mushrooms and broccoli tips and cook for just a few minutes – the vegetables must remain firm.
5 Cook the tagliatelle and drain.
6 Mix the pasta and sauce and add the vegetables.
7 Garnish with chopped coriander leaves.

Plum and Endive Salad

This is to accompany the recipe for Breast of Duck (see page 49).

•

SERVES 4

•

SALAD
leaves of curly endive, radicchio, lambs' lettuce, dandelion, as available
450 g/1 lb firm purple plums, cut in half and each half into three
5 spring onions, shredded lengthways and put into cold water to curl
50 g/2 oz mushrooms, finely sliced
a few leaves of basil
a few leaves of marjoram
crispy duck skins in curls for garnish (from Duck recipe page 49)

DRESSING
85 ml/3 fl oz hazelnut oil
25 ml/1 fl oz olive oil
50 ml/2 fl oz red wine vinegar
freshly ground pepper
¼ clove of garlic
½ tsp coarse-grain French mustard

•

1 Mix the dressing ingredients together.
2 Toss all the salad leaves, plums, spring onions, mushrooms and herbs in the dressing.
3 Garnish with the crispy duck skins.

Rhubarb Tart

SERVES 4–6
125 g/4 ½ oz flour
a pinch of salt
2 tbsp caster sugar
100 g/3 ½ oz butter
1 egg, separated
1 tsp lemon juice
icing sugar for topping
whipped cream to serve

FILLING
250 g/9 oz trimmed rhubarb (use young, red, thin stems)
75 g/2 ¾ oz caster sugar
2 egg yolks
75 g/2 ¾ oz butter
75 g/2 ¾ oz ground almonds
3 egg whites

•

1 Mix the flour, salt, sugar, butter, egg yolk and lemon juice together to make the pastry for the tart. Chill for at least 30 minutes.
2 Line a 20-cm/8-in flan tin with the pastry.
3 Bake 'blind' for about 10 minutes in the oven at 220°C/425°F/Gas Mark 7 and then thinly coat with the egg white and continue cooking until golden (about 5 minutes more).
4 Clean the rhubarb, chop into 5-mm/¼-in pieces and mix with half the caster sugar.
5 Mix the egg yolks, butter, remaining sugar and almonds together, then add the rhubarb mixture.
6 Whisk the egg whites until stiff and gently fold into the rhubarb mixture.
7 Pour the completed mixture into the pastry case and cook in the oven at 220°C/425°F/Gas Mark 7 for about 20 minutes or until golden.
8 Sprinkle the tart with icing sugar and serve warm with whipped cream.

Krumkaker

Biscuit Cups Filled with a Slightly-Frozen Cloudberry Ice Ceam, Cloudberry Liqueur and Spun Sugar

•

SERVES 4–6

•

BISCUIT (MAKES 8 CUPS)
2 eggs
85 g/3 oz caster sugar
125 g/4 ½ oz margarine
150 g/5 oz plain white flour
a pinch of freshly ground cardamom

FILLING
2 egg yolks
50 g/2 oz icing sugar
2 tbsp cloudberry liqueur
150 g/5 oz cloudberries
400 ml/14 fl oz double cream
1 egg white

•

SPUN SUGAR
150 g/5 oz caster sugar

•

1 To make the biscuit, mix the eggs and sugar until light and fluffy.
2 Melt the margarine and allow to cool.
3 Mix the sugar and eggs with the margarine, then add the flour and the cardamom – the mixture should have a thick spooning consistency.
4 The *krumkaker* (little biscuit cup) is cooked in an old-fashioned Norwegian double cast-iron mould (called a *krumkake jern*) which is heated over an open fire or on a cooker. There is a modern teflon-coated electrical appliance that does the same job. Cook the biscuits by spooning the mixture onto the hot iron and cooking until golden.
5 Quickly remove the cooked biscuits and shape into a cup.
6 To make the filling, mix the egg yolks and the icing sugar until pale and light. Add the liqueur and the cloudberries (leaving just a few for decoration).
7 Whip the cream; mix gently into the mixture.
8 Whip the egg white until stiff and gently fold into the mixture.
9 Freeze the mixture until it is the consistency of slightly soft ice cream.
10 For the spun sugar, melt the sugar in a non-stick pan until it is golden. Remove from the heat.
11 Wearing rubber gloves to protect your hands from the heat, draw fine threads of sugar from the pan using a wooden spoon. Wrap the threads of sugar around your hands in all directions to give a spun effect.
12 To serve, fill the *krumkaker* with ice cream. Decorate with cloudberries and spun sugar.

Paul Gayler

Paul Gayler made an early and intrepid start to his career — while his schoolmates studied chemistry he opted for cookery, along with forty-two girls and only one other male ally. He had a good time until he started coming top of the class, which didn't suit the girls of Marley School, Dagenham; but it did suit Paul's parents. Although his father was by profession a draughtsman, Stan and Lilian Gayler were gradually building up their own catering business, and every Saturday Paul and his mother prepared wedding breakfasts.

It was a logical step for Paul to take a course at the local technical college, and from there he went to the Palace Hotel, Torquay, to put theory into practice. Paul left in 1974 and moved to the Royal Garden Hotel, where he stayed for five years.

Five years ago, while we were filming Anton Mosimann, the Head Chef at the Dorchester, Paul was working there as his *sous chef*; which in practice, of course, meant he held the kitchen together in Anton's absence. It was from Anton Mosimann that Paul learned the grammar of plate service and the beauty of nouvelle cuisine, in Dorchester style: vegetables always at 10 o'clock and potatoes at 2 o'clock on the plate, with any meat 'smiling' in the front.

When Paul moved to Inigo Jones in Garrick Street, Covent Garden in 1983 as a director and Head Chef, he took the philosophy of the plate with him – and the freedom to develop his own style. And what style! *The Good Food Guide* acknowledges: 'As a stylist he's perhaps the most accomplished in Britain today', and there is no doubt, the plates at Inigo Jones are exquisite. Each dish has its own setting – feathery sprigs of coriander, baton carrots (Paul needs 720 for dinner servings alone), turned mushrooms, parcels of spinach, a spaghetti of celery. All these are labour-intensive details which make his vegetable section so crucial to the service. Here fish, meat and sauce sections converge for the final dressage. Perhaps it's just as well that customers can't see the time and care taken with each plate – if they could it would make their first incisions into this edible canvas seem an act of sacrilege.

'At its worst it is designer food, but at its best it is stunning, ' continues *The Good Food Guide*, still not sure what its feelings are about nouvelle cuisine. But Paul Gayler is the chef other chefs respect, for not hiding behind this label but rather championing its reverence for presentation and eclectic tastes. 'Nouvelle cuisine you may call it – but really it is just my style of cooking. I can't be doing with raspberries with mackerel or lobster served with vanilla. I'm simply bringing up to date the ingredients chefs used years ago.'

On the face of it, cooking doesn't seem to fit the image of Paul Gayler, and still less does the fastidious dressage of nouvelle cuisine. A short, dark, 32-year-old cockney with a no-nonsense East End approach, Paul is a bit of a loner in chef circles. Outside working hours he likes to go home and spend time with his wife, Anita, and his three young children; but apart from the family commitment, his obsession is food. He never wanted to be anything else but a cook and, as he says, it's just as well he's obsessed: 'Who else would leave home by coach from Benfleet at 7.15 a.m. and crawl back into bed at 2 a.m. only to get up again four hours later?' He does this five days a week.

Paul's mind is always at work, combining new ingredients in his head and working out new dishes. The number of ingredients in some dishes is quite staggering: a hot crispy confit of duck (which itself has a complicated marinade of ginger, cinnamon, cloves, nutmeg, coriander, garlic and mixed spice) rests on a mixed salad on top of an onion marmalade (made with shredded onion marinaded in red wine, honey and grenadine) and then sprinkled before serving with a vinaigrette of rosemary.

Not surprisingly in the kitchen of a devotee of nouvelle cuisine, there is a long line of homemade vinegars – prune, raspberry, blackberry, mushroom, sherry, and tea, made with Darjeeling tea and white wine vinegar which has been boiled and left to infuse for four weeks, then is passed through muslin. Tea vinegar is a perfect marinade for scallops. Paul smokes his own fish and bacon, duck and rabbit, and the flavours this yields are worth the stinging eyes everyone gets when the kitchen fills with smoke. He has even considered smoking vegetables – one idea he favours is smoked potatoes flavoured with cumin.

Though Paul doesn't want Inigo Jones to be labelled as a vegetarian restaurant, his vegetables are quite remarkable, whether as garnishes or as the main dish. Consider the ingenuity of a ravioli of celeriac: a large celeriac is peeled and finely sliced, then blanched and refreshed. Using the flat slice as a base, langoustines or scallops or vegetables are used as stuffing and a second slice is sandwiched on to the first, sealed with a mixture of egg yolk and cornflour. The resulting parcel is then cut into ravioli shapes. Courgette millefeuille, an elaborate garnish, is similarly impressive – courgettes sliced on the cross and singed with a hot iron, then sandwiched together with ratatouille.

Paul is keen to provide a series of individual flavours in his dishes, so that as you make your way around the plate you continually explore different tastes. A dish of poached quails' eggs – one white, one reddened by red wine, with spinach mousse and little oysters wrapped in a fresh spinach leaf, and all served with a red wine *jus* based on veal and fish – provides a subtle combination of meat, fish, eggs and vegetables.

The *Menu Potager* at Inigo Jones is, as far as I can tell, unique in a restaurant of this class. Paul has responded to customers' needs by providing four or five courses exclusively of vegetables – including the stock for the sauces. You might care to start with a salad of asparagus, watercress, avocado and herbs, followed by a warm mousseline of spinach with wild mushrooms, served with a truffle sauce. After that a lasagne of Niçoise vegetables; then goats' cheese and prunes baked in a thin pastry. And if you've room there's a pudding of chilled terrine of fruits marinated in Kirsch; but if you insist on a vegetable dessert, Paul can provide a '*quatre épices* sorbet with a carrot and orange sauce'!

Paul finds it challenging to produce a balanced menu using only vegetables. Varying textures become extremely important – he will not follow one cream sauce with another, and debates whether to follow spinach mousse with asparagus. When Paul started in Torquay as a *commis*, the head chef didn't want to share the special recipes with him, even though he was expected to reproduce them in the kitchen. Paul, however, gets enormous pleasure from the successes of his chefs, and is keen for them to enter competitions. Judges don't taste the dishes, which are set firmly in aspic – cooking standards are assumed to be high and judging is on presentation only.

Is this heresy? Can presentation be that important? Paul Gayler thinks it is at least half the value of the dish. 'A chef is a chef – and shouldn't be entering competitions unless he can cook to a high standard. And don't tell me a judge can taste thirty rum babas and come to any serious conclusion about a winner. We are in a creative industry – so let's see what we can create and how we present it. That's what cooking is all about.'

Paul Gayler

Sorbet de Thym Citroné et du Céleri PAGE 68

Bisque de Lièvre aux Lentilles et Madère

Creamed Hare Soup with Lentils and Madeira
•
SERVES 4–6
•

1 fresh hare, skinned and cleaned (retain blood)
100 g/3 ½ oz lentils
50 g/2 oz carrots
3 shallots
white of ½ leek
½ stick of celery
1 clove of garlic
bay leaf
thyme
cloves
salt and pepper
70 ml/2 ½ fl oz white wine
150 ml/ ¼ pt Madeira
125 g/4 ½ oz butter
½ tbsp tomato purée
1.5 l/2 ½ pt water
70 ml/2 ½ fl oz double cream
chervil for garnish
•

Ideally, steps 1–3 should be done the day before the soup is to be made.

1 Soak the lentils in cold water for 12 hours.

2 Remove the saddle from the hare, leaving it whole, and cut up the remaining meat into 2.5-cm/1-in pieces. Place all in a large bowl.

3 Add the vegetables, including the garlic, all finely chopped; add the bay leaf, thyme, cloves and seasoning. Pour on the white wine and half the Madeira and leave to marinate for 12 hours.

4 Remove the hare and vegetables from the marinade and drain well in a colander. Remove the fillets from the saddle and place to one side.

5 In a thick-bottomed saucepan, fry the hare pieces and saddle bones to seal in 50 g/2 oz of the butter; add the remaining marinade and tomato purée. Add the water and bring to the boil. Add the lentils, cover and cook gently for 45 minutes.

6 In the mean time, heat the remaining butter and fry the hare fillets for 8–10 minutes, keeping them pink. Allow to rest while you finish the soup.

7 When the soup is cooked, pass it firstly through a coarse strainer, then through a fine sieve, to remove any bone fragments from the hare.

8 Beat the hare blood with a little water, add to the soup, and simmer for 1–2 minutes on a gentle heat. Pass the soup through the fine strainer again, add the cream and the remaining Madeira.

9 Slice the hare fillets into neat medallions and arrange in a circle in a soup plate. Pour on the hot soup, garnish with a little chervil and serve.

Soupe de Choux et Huîtres au Cumin

Cabbage and Oyster Broth Flavoured with Cumin
•
SERVES 4–5
¼ medium white cabbage
12 small native oysters
25 g/1 oz butter
1 tsp cumin seed
1 l/1 ¾ pt chicken stock
salt and pepper
double cream to taste
•

1 Remove the outer leaves from the cabbage, cut it into 1-cm/½-in dice and wash well.

2 Melt the butter in a saucepan, then sweat the cabbage under a lid until soft without colouring. Add the cumin seed and mix well.

3 Pour on the chicken stock, bring to the boil, skim and allow to simmer until cooked.

4 Meanwhile, open the oysters, remove from their shells, and filter the juices carefully through a fine muslin cloth to remove any grit or sand. Also remove the muscle, as this is rather tough.

5 Add the strained oyster juice to the soup, adjust the seasoning and add the double cream to taste.

6 Pour the soup over the oysters in serving bowls.

Rillettes d'Agneau au Genièvre at au Romarin

Lamb Pâté Flavoured with Juniper and Rosemary

•

SERVES 12 AS AN HORS D'OEUVRE

1.5 kg/3–3 ½ lb lean shoulder of lamb
550 g/1 ¼ lb fillet of pork
300 g/11 oz pork fat
550 g/1 ¼ lb lamb fat
600 ml/1 pt water
2 carrots
1 onion
3 cloves of garlic (in skin)
2 level tbsp juniper berries
a small bunch of rosemary
bouquet garni (leek, celery, thyme and bay leaf)
300 ml/ ½ pt dry white wine
salt and pepper
a little nutmeg
24 large cos lettuce leaves, blanched
onion, beetroot and gherkins, shredded, to garnish

•

HERB VINAIGRETTE

1 tsp Dijon mustard
4 tbsp Jerez sherry vinegar
8 tbsp peanut oil
8 tbsp olive oil
25 g/1 oz fresh herbs (tarragon, chervil, chives), finely chopped
salt and pepper

•

1 Cube the pork and lamb fat and place in a pan. Pour on the water, cover and heat slowly until the fat melts.

2 Put the meats, also cut into cubes, in the pan. Add the carrots, onion, garlic, juniper berries, herbs and half the white wine.

3 Lightly season, cover and cook in the oven at 180°C/350°F/Gas Mark 4 for 4 hours, or until the liquid has almost completely evaporated.

4 Remove from the oven, discard the garlic, herbs and vegetables, and place the pan on a high heat, slowly stirring until the meat is broken up

and evaporation is complete. Do not boil.

5 Add the remaining white wine, remove from the heat and allow to cool. Season with a little salt, pepper and nutmeg. When completely cold, lay out the blanched lettuce leaves; fill each leaf with some of the lamb *rillette* mixture and fold into small balls or rolls, allowing two per person.

6 To make the herb vinaigrette, whisk together the mustard, vinegar and oils to form an emulsion, add the fresh herbs and season to taste.

7 To serve, place two *rillettes* on each plate, cordon with a little of the vinaigrette and garnish with a small salad of shredded onion, beetroot and gherkins. Serve well chilled.

Raviolis de Pommes de Terre, Foie Gras et aux Girolles

Potato and Foie Gras Ravioli with Wild Mushrooms

•

SERVES 4–6 AS AN HORS D'OEUVRE

275 g/10 oz new potatoes
115 g/4 oz cooked foie gras (preferably fresh)
85 g/3 oz butter
1 large shallot
2 tbsp fresh mixed herbs (tarragon, chervil and chives), finely chopped
salt and pepper
400 g/14 oz fresh spinach
1 tbsp thyme leaves
1 tbsp fresh chervil
25 g/1 oz fresh girolles (wild mushrooms)
150 ml/ ¼ pt double cream
nutmeg
150 ml/ ¼ pt butter sauce (see Cocotte d'Artichaut recipe on page 67)

•

RAVIOLI PASTE

250 g/9 oz flour
120 ml/4 fl oz water
30 ml/1 ¼ fl oz oil
¼ tsp salt
beaten egg for egg wash

1 Prepare the ravioli paste: place the flour in a bowl, make a well in the centre, pour in the water and oil, add seasoning and amalgamate to form a paste. Allow to rest for at least 1 hour.

2 Prepare the filling: clean the new potatoes well and cook in their skins in boiling water. Allow to go cold, peel off the skins and dice the potatoes finely. Melt 50 g/2 oz of the butter in a pan, add the shallot, finely chopped, the mixed fresh herbs and the potatoes, and mix gently together without breaking up. Season to taste and allow to cool thoroughly. Dice the foie gras into 5-mm/¼-in pieces, mix with the potatoes, adjust the seasoning and place to one side.

3 Blanch the spinach in boiling water, refresh in iced water and dry in a clean cloth. Place in a liquidizer to obtain a thick spinach purée.

4 Roll out the dough into thin sheets (preferably through a pasta machine), lay out on a board and, using a 7.5-cm/3-in biscuit cutter, cut rounds in the paste. Egg-wash the perimeter of each round and place a spoonful of the potato and foie gras filling onto half the round; fold over the other side, pressing the edges to form a seal. Allow to rest in the refrigerator for 15 minutes before cooking.

5 Poach the ravioli in boiling water with a little oil and seasoning for 3–4 minutes, keeping them *al dente*. Drain off the water.

6 In a separate pan, using half the remaining butter, gently heat the ravioli, thyme and chervil.

7 In another pan, sauté the *girolles* in the rest of the butter.

8 To serve, reheat the spinach purée, add the double cream and a little butter, season with salt, pepper and nutmeg. Place the purée in the centre of a serving plate with the ravioli on top and scatter the *girolles* overall. Finish with a cordon of butter sauce around the purée, and serve immediately.

Panache de Tous les Poissons au Vin Rouge et à la Moelle

Assortment of Steamed Fish in Red Wine Anchovy Sauce with Meat Marrow

•

SERVES 4

2 × 200-g/7-oz red mullet
1 × 400-g/14-oz sea bass
1 × 350-g/12-oz Dover sole
1 × 200-g/7-oz piece of turbot
1 × 200-g/7-oz fillet of monkfish
8 fresh scallops
2 shallots
85 g/3 oz butter
150 ml/¼ pt red wine
1 l/1 ¾ pt veal stock
marrow from 2 big bones
6 fresh anchovies or *2 tsp anchovy essence*
a sprig of thyme
bay leaf
peppercorns
600 ml/1 pt water
2 tbsp double cream
sprigs of thyme for garnish

•

1 To prepare the red wine sauce, slice the shallots and sauté in a little of the butter. Add the red wine and bring to the boil. Cook until reduced by half, then skim well. Add the veal stock, and reduce by half again. Strain and reserve.

2 Prepare the fish: clean the mullet, sea bass and sole, removing all bones. Trim the remaining fish. Keep all trimmings and bones to one side to add to the sauce. Cut the fish into 85-g/3-oz pieces.

3 Remove the meat marrow from the bone by smashing it with a heavy knife or meat cleaver, taking care to keep each marrow in one piece. (The butcher can do this for you.) Soak the marrow in cold water to remove all traces of blood.

4 Pass the fresh anchovies through water to remove excess salt content, remove the head and bones, and press through a fine sieve to obtain a fresh anchovy purée. Alternatively, use anchovy essence.

5 Chop the fish bones and sauté in a little butter with the thyme, bay leaf and crushed peppercorns. Moisten with the water and bring to the boil, skimming often. Cook for 10 minutes.

6 Pass through a sieve and reduce by half. Add the red wine sauce, season, then add the cream, remaining butter and anchovy purée. Strain.

7 Gently poach the meat marrow in water for 10 seconds; cut into eight slices 1 cm/1 in thick.

8 Season the fish and cook in a fish steamer or poach until heated through, starting with the firmer fish, i.e. Dover sole, turbot etc.

9 Pour the anchovy sauce onto a plate, and arrange the fish on it. Garnish with marrow and thyme.

Safrane de Langoustines aux Nouilles Fraîches et aux Légumes

Dublin Bay Prawns in a Creamed Saffron Orange Sauce with Noodles

•

SERVES 4

24 fresh, uncooked langoustines (Dublin Bay prawns)
100 g/3 ½ oz butter
50 g/2 oz mirepoix (finely chopped onion, carrot, garlic and parsley)
70 ml/2 ½ fl oz dry white wine
70 ml/2 ½ fl oz Sauterne wine
600 ml/1 pt fish stock
300 ml/ ½ pt double cream
1 tsp fresh saffron
salt and pepper
a little fresh chervil for garnish

•

FRESH NOODLES

200 g/7 oz flour
2 eggs
2 egg yolks
1 tbsp olive oil
1 tbsp water
salt

VEGETABLE NOODLES

50 g/2 oz courgettes
50 g/2 oz carrots
1 small leek
1 orange

•

1 Prepare the fresh noodles: place the flour in a bowl and make a well in the centre. Break in the eggs, add the yolks, olive oil, water and salt, and mix the flour in towards the centre to amalgamate all the ingredients into a paste. Rest for 2 hours.

2 Carefully peel the langoustines. Place the shells in a bowl and smash them with a mortar.

3 Place a little of the butter in a pan, add the *mirepoix* and sweat it gently without colouring. Add the crushed shells and sauté them together. Pour in the wines and cook until reduced by half.

4 Add the previously prepared fish stock and reduce again by half. Add the double cream, reduce again until thickened, and add the saffron. Pass through a fine muslin cloth.

5 Prepare the vegetable noodles: using a fine slicer (or mandoline), cut the courgettes and carrots into fine slices lengthways, then cut in half again to make noodle-width. Cut the leek finely by hand.

6 Peel the orange and cut the peel into fine strips. Extract all the juice from the orange.

7 Blanch the vegetable noodles and orange strips and refresh in iced water to keep crisp.

8 Roll out the fresh noodles, using the noodle attachment on a pasta machine. Cook them in boiling water with salt and a drop of olive oil for 1–2 minutes until *al dente*.

9 Drain the noodles and heat them in a little butter with the vegetables and orange strips.

10 Season the langoustines and steam them for 3 minutes.

11 Place the langoustines on a serving plate to form a circle. Place the noodles in the centre, showing the different colours.

12 Finish the sauce with the orange juice and remaining butter, and cordon the sauce around the langoustines. Garnish with fresh chervil and serve immediately.

Waterzooï de Poularde aux Moules à l'Anis

Ragout of Chicken and Mussels in a Basil and Aniseed Sauce

•

SERVES 4

4 × 175-g/6-oz breasts of chicken
1 l/1 ¾ pt fresh mussels (in shells)
50 g/2 oz butter
25 g/1 oz shallots
1 tbsp parsley stalks
150 ml/ ¼ pt white wine
600 ml/1 pt chicken stock
a little olive oil
1 leek
2 carrots
1 stick of celery
1 small fennel
3 tomatoes, blanched, peeled, de-seeded and diced
1 clove of garlic, crushed
1 tbsp thyme leaves
1 bay leaf
salt and pepper
70 ml/2 ½ fl oz Pernod or Ricard
150 ml/ ¼ pt double cream
6 fresh basil leaves

•

1 Scrub the mussels and wash well (discard any that are broken or open and do not shut immediately when tapped).

2 Lightly butter a pan, put in the shallots, roughly chopped, and parsley stalks and place the mussels on top. Moisten with the white wine and half the chicken stock.

3 Place on the heat, cover with a lid and steam until the mussel shells open, about 1 minute.

4 Pour the mussels into a colander, set over a bowl and allow to cool. Reserve the liquid.

5 Clean the mussels, removing the beards. Strain the cooking liquid to remove sand and shell fragments.

6 Place a little butter and olive oil in another pan. Add the leek, carrots, celery and fennel, all finely diced, and the tomatoes, garlic, thyme and bay leaf. Sweat together, covered, for 2–3 minutes.

7 Remove the lid, season the chicken breasts and place on top. Moisten with the Pernod or Ricard, pour on the mussel stock and add the remaining chicken stock. Cover with buttered paper and poach gently for 8–10 minutes or until cooked.

8 Take out the chicken breasts and keep them warm.

9 Boil the cooking liquor until reduced by half, add the double cream and reduce until thickened. Finish by adding the remaining butter in pieces to give a thick, smooth sauce.

10 Cut the chicken into small escalopes and place on a plate. Add the mussels to the sauce, reheat without boiling, season and add the basil leaves, finely shredded. Pour over the chicken and serve immediately.

Cotelette de Pigeonneau au Ris de Veau à la Lie de Porto

Cutlet of Pigeon and Veal Sweetbreads with Port Lees Sauce

•

SERVES 4

2 Norfolk squab pigeons
8 medallions veal sweetbreads, blanched, cleaned and sautéed in butter
100 g/3 ½ oz large shallots, chopped
25 g/1 oz butter
100 ml/3 ½ fl oz white wine
100 g/3 ½ oz lean pork
85 g/3 oz unsalted bacon fat
liver, heart and lung from the pigeons
100 g/3 ½ oz chicken livers
salt and pepper
nutmeg
4 large pieces dry pigs' caul (crépinette)

•

MARINADE

25 ml/1 fl oz port
25 ml/1 fl oz cognac
25 ml/1 fl oz olive oil

SAUCE

pigeon carcass
3 tbsp oil
85 g/3 oz mirepoix (carrot, onion and
celery, finely chopped)
150 ml/ ¼ pt red wine
600 ml/1 pt veal stock
a few sprigs of thyme
bay leaf
peppercorns
juniper berries
150 ml/ ¼ pt port
2 tbsp port lees (sediment from old port)
25 g/1 oz butter

•

1 Remove the legs and breast from the pigeons and skin. Remove the thighs at the joint for use in the stuffing. Marinate the breasts and drumsticks in port, cognac and olive oil for 30 minutes.

2 Prepare the stuffing: sweat the shallots in a little butter, pour in the white wine and reduce by half. Cool. Remove any sinew from the meat and mince the pork, bacon fat, the pigeon thighs, offal and chicken livers with the shallots. Pass through a fine sieve and season with salt, pepper and nutmeg.

3 Spread a 5-mm/ ¼-in layer of stuffing mixture on the caul and place two medallions on this, then lay the pigeon breast on top and place the drumstick at the tip of the breast to resemble a cutlet in shape. Cover with more stuffing. Fold over the caul to enclose. Chill.

4 Chop the pigeon carcass and fry in the hot oil with the *mirepoix* until nicely browned. Pour in the red wine and cook until reduced by two-thirds. Add the veal stock, herbs, peppercorns and juniper berries, and simmer gently for 30 minutes, skimming. Pass through a muslin cloth.

5 Lightly sauté the cutlets in butter, until coloured. Cook at 200°C/400°F/Gas Mark 6 for 5 minutes. Take out and keep warm.

6 Add the port wine to the juices in the pan and cook until reduced by half. Pour on the prepared sauce and cook for a few minutes, skimming constantly. Pass through a fine muslin cloth, finish with the port lees and a knob of butter.

Choucroute de Navets aux Pommes Douces

Turnip Choucroute with Apple

•

SERVES 4

1.5 kg/3 lb large turnips
15 g/ ½ oz coarse salt
2 tbsp black peppercorns
12 juniper berries
50 g/2 oz lard or goose fat
1 large onion, finely sliced
1 tbsp cumin seeds
300 ml/ ½ pt dry white Alsatian wine
1 l/1 ¾ pt vegetable stock
salt and pepper
2 cooking apples

•

1 Peel the turnips and grate them coarsely.

2 Place a fine layer of shredded turnip in an earthenware crock or bowl. Lightly sprinkle with a little coarse salt, peppercorns and juniper berries. Repeat the layers, ending with turnip.

3 Cover with a clean cloth, and a piece of wood or plate and a heavy weight. Leave overnight.

4 The following day, heat the lard or goose fat in a thick-bottomed pan, add the finely sliced onion and brown lightly, then add the cumin and cook together for a couple of minutes.

5 Remove the juniper berries and peppercorns from the shredded turnip. Place the turnip in a colander and rinse thoroughly under cold water. Dry in a clean cloth and add to the pan.

6 Pour the Alsatian wine and vegetable stock into the pan so the liquid level covers two-thirds of the ingredients. Lightly season with salt and pepper, cover with a lid, and cook in the oven at 160°C/325°F/Gas Mark 3 for 1–1½ hours, by which time all the liquid should have evaporated.

7 Peel the apples and remove the cores, grate them finely and add to the turnips. Blend well and allow to cool.

8 To serve, reheat the *choucroute* in a little butter. It is a particularly good accompaniment to venison or pigeon.

Nems de Céleri-Rave à l'Orientale PAGE 64

Paul Gayler

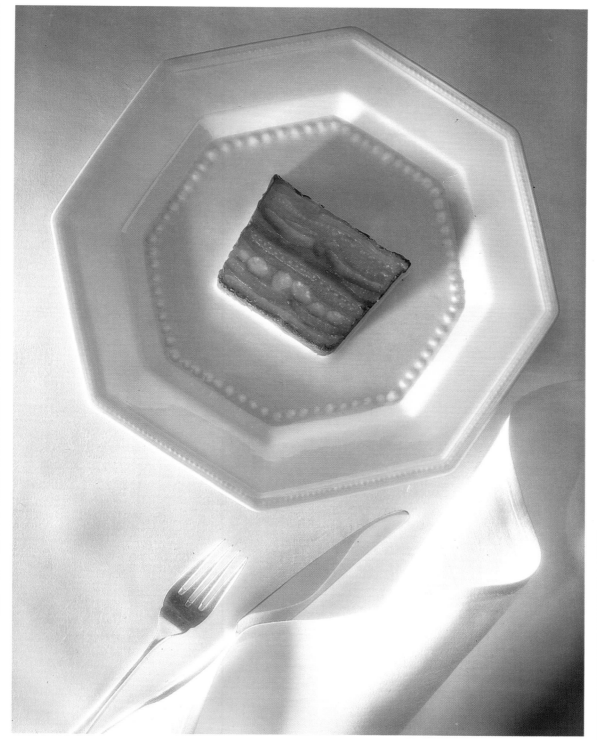

Terrine de Ratatouille Niçoise PAGE 65

Nems de Céleri-Rave à l'Orientale

Celeriac Spring Pancake Rolls with Chinese Vegetables

•

SERVES 4

2 medium-large celeriacs
a squeeze of lemon juice
25 g/1 oz mouli (Chinese radish)
¼ red pepper
¼ green pepper
¼ yellow pepper
2 carrots
25 g/1 oz beansprouts
3 spring onions
25 g/1 oz mange-tout
a little sesame oil
25 g/1 oz butter
¼ tsp crushed garlic
a small piece of root ginger
2 egg yolks
4 tbsp arrowroot
4 tbsp clarified butter
fresh coriander leaves for garnish

•

TOMATO CORIANDER SAUCE

50 g/2 oz butter
2 shallots, finely chopped
2 cloves of garlic, crushed
4 tomatoes
1 tbsp tomato purée
70 ml/2 ½ fl oz sherry vinegar
150 ml/ ¼ pt white wine
300 ml/ ½ pt water
2 tbsp soy sauce
10 fresh coriander leaves

•

1 Peel the celeriacs and slice them into very thin rounds, preferably on a slicing machine.
2 Blanch the celeriac in lemon-acidulated boiling water (boiling water to which fresh lemon juice has been added) for 10 seconds, then plunge into iced water to refresh.
3 Remove and dry on a clean cloth.

4 For the filling, finely shred all the other vegetables. Heat the butter and the sesame oil in a frying pan. Add the crushed garlic, then the shredded vegetables and the ginger. Cook for 2–3 minutes, keeping the vegetables crisp.
5 Remove the ingredients from the pan and allow to cool.
6 Prepare the celeriac pancake rolls: place two circles of celeriac overlapping on a clean surface. If using smaller celeriacs, you may need several circles. Bind the egg yolks and arrowroot together to form a paste and brush this mixture lightly around the edge of the celeriac circles.
7 Place a portion of Chinese vegetables in the centre of the celeriac circles, then roll up the four edges to the centre to form a pancake roll. Leave in the refrigerator for 30 minutes to set. Allow two rolls per person as a first course.

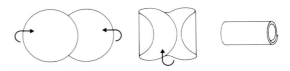

8 Prepare the sauce: put the butter, shallots, and garlic in a pan and cook together without colouring. Add the tomatoes, roughly chopped, and the tomato purée, and cook for a further 5 minutes.
9 Add the sherry vinegar and white wine and cook until reduced by half. Pour in the water, cover with a lid and cook gently for 20 minutes.
10 When ready, pass the sauce through a fine sieve. Finish by adding the soy sauce and the coriander leaves, finely shredded.
11 Fry the celeriac pancake rolls in the clarified butter until golden. Arrange two on a serving plate and pour a little of the coriander and tomato sauce alongside.
12 Garnish with fresh coriander leaves and serve immediately.

Smaller versions of these rolls make excellent hot canapes.

Terrine de Ratatouille Niçoise

SERVES 10–12

20 large spinach leaves, blanched and refreshed
salt and pepper
3 red peppers
3 yellow peppers
2 green peppers
2 aubergines
1 fennel
6 medium courgettes
olive oil

•

MOUSSE

olive oil
½ onion
2 cloves of new season garlic, crushed
3 red peppers
2 tomatoes, chopped
2 tbsp tomato purée
12 basil leaves
a sprig of thyme
1 tbsp sugar
150 ml/ ¼ pt dry white wine
300 ml/ ½ pt water
10 leaves gelatine (soaked in cold water)

•

BASIL SAUCE

25 fresh basil leaves
150 ml/ ¼ pt mayonnaise
150 ml/ ¼ pt single cream
lemon juice to taste
salt and pepper

•

1 Line a terrine mould first with clingfilm, then line it with the spinach leaves, overlapping each other neatly without any gaps. Season lightly.

2 Prepare the vegetables as follows:

Peppers – cook in olive oil in the oven at 220°C/425°F/Gas Mark 7 for 20–25 minutes. Cool, then remove the skins and seeds.

Aubergines – cut into four lengthways. Cook in olive oil in the oven at 220°C/425°F/Gas Mark 7 for 20 minutes.

Fennel – peel and separate the layers and blanch in boiling water for 5–8 minutes. Refresh in iced water and dry.

Courgettes – cut into four lengthways and shape neatly into pencil thickness. Blanch and refresh, then dry.

3 Prepare the mousse: heat a little oil in a pan, add the onion, roughly chopped, and crushed garlic.

4 Cut the red peppers in half, remove the seeds and stalk. Chop roughly and add to the pan. Add the chopped tomatoes and tomato purée, herbs and sugar. Cook for 4–5 minutes.

5 Add the white wine and cook until reduced by half. Add the water and cook gently on the edge of the stove until the vegetables are well cooked, about 15–20 minutes.

6 When cooked, add the soaked gelatine, remove the pan from the heat and allow to cool.

7 Purée the mixture in a liquidizer, then pass the purée through a fine sieve. Allow to cool completely and adjust the seasoning.

8 Prepare the terrine: pour 2 tablespoons of mousse into the bottom of the spinach-lined mould, cut the yellow peppers to size and layer the terrine from end to end. Season between each layer.

9 Pour another 2 tablespoons of mousse on top, then add the aubergine, skin side down first to make a good colour contrast, then another 2 tablespoons of mousse followed by the courgettes. Repeat the process, alternating layers of mousse and vegetable in the following sequence: red pepper, fennel, green pepper, aubergine, yellow pepper. Finish with a layer of mousse.

10 Fold over the spinach leaves carefully to seal the terrine, then cover with clingfilm. Press the terrine with a weight for 8–24 hours in the refrigerator.

11 Prepare the basil sauce: place all the ingredients in a liquidizer and blend well. Adjust seasoning and consistency.

12 Pour a little sauce onto a plate, cut a slice of terrine and place it on the sauce. Garnish with some piped mayonnaise around the terrine for presentation. Serve chilled.

Paul Gayler

Cocotte d' Artichaut aux Champignons en Cage

Cocotte d'Artichaut aux Champignons en Cage

Baked Artichoke with Wild Mushrooms in Pastry with Vegetables

●

SERVES 4

4 large globe artichokes
100 g/3 ½ oz selection of wild mushrooms,
(depending upon seasonal availability – e.g.
morels, trompettes, mousserons St Georges, girolles)
100 g/3 ½ oz puff pastry
4 tbsp olive oil
4 lemons
2 shallots, finely chopped
butter
70 ml/2 ½ fl oz Madeira
70 ml/2 ½ fl oz white wine
150 ml/ ¼ pt double cream
salt and pepper
beaten egg for egg wash
a little clarified butter

●

VEGETABLE STOCK

¼ onion
½ leek
½ stick of celery
25 g/1 oz carrots
25 g/1 oz cabbage
100 g/3 ½ oz butter
¼ tsp crushed garlic
½ tsp crushed black peppercorns
1 tsp sea salt
150 ml/ ¼ pt white wine
300 ml/ ½ pt water
2 tbsp double cream

●

GARNISH

Select from the following to taste:
12 baby turnips, 12 water asparagus,
6 asparagus, 12 girolles,
8 cherry tomatoes, 12 baby carrots
butter
chervil

1 Prepare the vegetable stock: peel and finely dice the vegetables. Place 25 g/1 oz of butter in a pan and add the diced vegetables and garlic. Cook together, covered, for about 5 minutes until soft. Remove the lid and add the black peppercorns, a little sea salt and the white wine, and cook until reduced by half.

2 Add the water and bring to the boil, skimming frequently. Leave to cook slowly for 20–25 minutes on the edge of the heat. When cooked, pour the stock through a fine sieve. Place to one side. This stock can be kept in a refrigerator for 3–4 days.

3 Break the stalks off the artichokes and remove the outer leaves with a knife. Turn one artichoke to form an artichoke bottom and rub with lemon frequently to prevent browning. Remove the hairy choke in the centre with a spoon and rub with lemon. Prepare all four the same way.

4 Bring 300 ml/ ½ pt of water to the boil in a saucepan and add the olive oil and the juice of 2 lemons. Add the artichoke bottoms and cook for 8–10 minutes. Allow to cool in the liquid.

5 Prepare the filling for the artichokes by cooking the chopped shallots in a knob of butter, then add the washed selection of wild mushrooms. Cook together, and add the Madeira and white wine. Cook until reduced by half, then add the cream and continue reducing until the mushrooms are coated with the cream. Add a little cold butter and mix well. Adjust the seasoning and allow to cool.

6 Butter and season the artichoke bottoms. Fill each with a generous spoonful of the mushroom ragout.

7 Using a sharp knife cut four circles of puff pastry 6.5 cm/2 ½ in diameter. Make 1-cm/½-in gashes into the pastry at regular intervals in lines across the diameter (see next page).

8 Egg-wash the pastry and place one piece carefully on each artichoke, pulling downwards to form a trellis effect or cage. Trim the sides neatly on the underside of the artichoke. Place in the refrigerator for 2 hours to rest the pastry.

9 Egg-wash the cages and place in the oven at 200°C/400°F/Gas Mark 6 for 5–8 minutes.

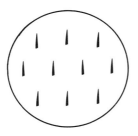

10 Cook the vegetables chosen for the garnish in a little water, butter and seasoning.

11 Make a sauce from the vegetable stock: cook the stock until reduced by half, add the double cream and reduce again until thickened. Finish with knobs of the remaining butter, added a little at a time to form an emulsion. Adjust the seasoning.

12 Pour a little sauce onto a serving plate, remove the artichoke from the oven and brush it with a little clarified butter for appearance. Arrange the selected vegetables attractively around the edge of the plate, place the artichoke in the centre, garnish with freshly picked chervil and serve immediately.

1 Boil the sugar, water and glucose together, remove from the heat and add the lemon thyme and celery leaves, then finally the soaked gelatine.

2 Add the lemon juice and the vodka, if used, and allow to cool.

3 Pass the whole through a fine strainer and pour into a sorbet machine. Turn on the machine and freeze to the correct soft consistency. If you do not have a sorbet machine, put the mixture in a container in the freezer compartment at the coldest setting until half frozen. Then beat in a cold bowl or work in a food processor until smooth. Return to the container and freeze until firm.

4 To serve, either use an ice cream scoop or form the sorbet into *quenelle* shapes with a tablespoon. Place the sorbet in a chilled glass, and garnish with a sprig of fresh lemon thyme and a celery leaf.

Sorbet de Thym Citroné et du Céleri

Lemon Thyme and Celery Sorbet

•

MAKES 1L/1¾PT

10 sprigs of fresh lemon thyme
8–10 leaves of branch celery
225 g/8 oz sugar
450 ml/¾ pt water
50 g/2 oz glucose
½ leaf gelatine (soaked in water)
300 ml/½ pt lemon juice (freshly squeezed)
45 ml/1½ fl oz vodka (optional)
sprigs of fresh lemon thyme and celery leaves
for garnish

Entremet Moscovite de Rhubarbe aux Fruits Rouges

Chilled Mousseline of Rhubarb with Red Fruits, Raspberry Sauce and Almond Biscuit

•

SERVES 8–10

•

RHUBARB PURÉE

250 g/9 oz cleaned rhubarb
65–70 ml/2½ fl oz water
65 g/2½ oz sugar

•

RHUBARB MOSCOVITE

250 g/9 oz cooked rhubarb purée (from the above)
2 leaves gelatine
70 g/2¼ oz caster sugar
2 egg yolks
250 g/9 oz double cream, lightly whipped

•

RASPBERRY SAUCE

250 g/9 oz fresh raspberries
125 g/4½ oz sugar
juice of ½ lemon

ALMOND BISCUIT

100 g/3 ½ oz flaked or nibbed almonds
3 egg whites
125 g/4 ½ oz caster sugar
25 g/1 oz flour
40 g/1 ½ oz melted butter

•

DECORATION

a selection of fresh summer fruits
a few leaves of mint

•

1 Make the rhubarb purée: cook all the ingredients together, liquidize and pass through a coarse strainer.

2 Make the rhubarb moscovite: soak the gelatine in cold water. Heat the rhubarb purée with 30 g/1 ¼ oz of the sugar. Cream the egg yolks with the rest of the sugar, then add the boiling rhubarb purée. Return the mixture to a clean pan and cook over a very low heat until it thickens. Add the gelatine and pass through a fine strainer. Stir occasionally until the mixture thickens and becomes cool, then lightly fold in the whipped cream. Pour into individual moulds.

3 Prepare the raspberry sauce: liquidize the fresh raspberries and pass them through a sieve. Boil the sugar, covered, with a little water, to a temperature of 116°C/240°F (soft boil), add the raspberry purée and bring back to the boil. Skim, pass through a fine strainer, and add lemon juice.

4 Prepare the biscuit: beat the egg whites and sugar together until well combined. Add the almonds and flour and mix thoroughly. Pour in melted butter and leave to rest. Spoon onto greased trays and press out with a wet fork. Bake in the oven at 150°C/300°F/Gas Mark 2 until golden brown – about 4–5 minutes. Lift the biscuits and lay them over a rolling pin to give a crescent shape.

5 To serve, pour a little raspberry sauce onto each plate, place a mousse on top and accompany with an almond biscuit. Decorate with a selection of fresh fruits in season, such as raspberries, strawberries, blackcurrants, redcurrants, wild strawberries, and a mint leaf.

Parfait Glacé aux Avelines, Clouté d'Ananas Confit

Iced Parfait of Hazelnuts Studded with Pineapple and Blackcurrant-Kirsch Sauce

•

SERVES 10–12

100 g/3 ½ oz ground hazelnuts
175 g/6 oz sugar
150 ml/¼ pt milk
10 egg yolks
500 ml/18 fl oz double cream
½ small pineapple, cut in very small dice and cooked in sugar water until very soft

•

SAUCE

250 g/9 oz blackcurrant purée
125 g/4 ½ oz sugar
4 tbsp Kirsch

•

DECORATION

whole hazelnuts
100 g/3 ½ oz fresh blackcurrants
4 mint leaves

•

1 Put the sugar and milk in a saucepan and bring to the boil, then allow to cool. Add the egg yolks, then place the saucepan in a shallow water bath containing enough water to come halfway up the saucepan. Cook this mixture for 1 hour, stirring occasionally. It should become very thick.

2 Take the mixture off the heat, pour into a food mixer and beat thoroughly until cooled and approximately double the volume.

3 When cold, fold in the ground hazelnuts, the whipped cream and finally the pineapple confit; blend well together.

4 Pour into individual moulds (or into a terrine) and place in the freezer overnight.

5 To make the sauce, liquidize the ingredients together and pour through a fine strainer.

6 Turn out the parfait and decorate with the whole hazelnuts. Set the parfait on a base of blackcurrant-Kirsch sauce, decorate with mint leaves and the blackcurrants. Serve chilled.

Franco Taruschio

Franco and Ann Taruschio spent their honeymoon scrubbing the floors of a broken-down coaching inn they'd bought with all but 3s 9d of their savings. The Walnut Tree on the windy road to Abergavenny in sight of Skirrid Fawr, a local mountain with Satanic connections, wasn't exactly an auspicious location in 1963. And that first year was incredibly difficult. The local doctor would perhaps come for lunch once a week but that was about it, until Christmas when a local family asked them to cook Christmas lunch for twelve. It was a wonderful break although, even pooling their wedding presents, Ann and Franco just didn't have enough crockery or cutlery for twelve – but they did have a large and rather beautiful Georgian table. Somehow they managed, and word got around that food was good at the Walnut Tree. Today they serve hundreds of people every day, in the bar, the bistro, or in the evening, in the little restaurant. 'Queues usually form outside before the doors even open,' said *The Good Food Guide* in 1984 – which is hardly surprising as Franco has attracted consistently good notices in the guide from the early seventies.

If serving Italian food in the Welsh valleys seems an odd sort of 'marriage', Franco was prepared for the rural setting at least, since his parents farmed in Montefano, near Ancona, in Italy. Franco trained at the Bellagio Hotel School on Lake Como and then worked in hotels in Switzerland and France before coming to England to the Three Horseshoes Hotel in Rugby. There he met his wife, Ann, an art teacher whose love for Italy until that time had been purely theoretical.

When they moved to the Walnut Tree in 1963, the Welsh valleys were attracting second-home owners like Edna O'Brien and Terence Stamp, who brought with them a demand for sophisticated food. And while Mary Quant was altering our looks, Elizabeth David was certainly inspiring, if not radically changing, our eating habits.

Franco has cleverly combined Italian and Welsh dishes. Oysters, for example, are served with laverbread instead of spinach, and Welsh lamb is enhanced by herbs and spices, making it similar to *Arosto d'Abbacchio* – a young suckling lamb spit-roasted with rosemary.

But there's a third and very strong influence on Franco's cooking and that comes from their adopted daughter, Pavini. This 'gracious lady', as her name means, who is now 10, was left by her mother with the nuns of an orphanage in Bangkok and later adopted by Ann and Franco, after a complicated legal tangle, when she was four months old. Together with the Walnut Tree, she is the centre of their lives. They are both keen to foster in Pavini a sense of her own culture – so it's just as well that Franco loves Thai flavours. The combination of lemon grass and kaffir quite literally gives him the 'judders – so maybe it is an aphrodisiac'. Staff lunches now almost always have a Thai influence, and some of the ideas have made it onto the actual menu – like the Thai mussels (cooked in garlic, chilli and mint) or the Thai pork appetiser (minced pork with peanuts, garlic, coriander, shallots and sugar).

Franco Taruschio

There's a tremendous sense of involvement at the Walnut Tree – from staff, suppliers, and customers too. The staff and suppliers seem to relish the challenge of a sophisticated menu; the suppliers provide the very best of ingredients, while the kitchen staff use them to interpret Franco's wishes. It's hard to imagine the early days of the Walnut Tree when Franco just couldn't attract staff: 'Absolutely no one wanted to work in this inn in the middle of nowhere.' But once they came they stayed – like Anna, an Italian woman married to a Welshman who has found a home from home at the Walnut Tree; she has been washing up and making pasta and ice cream for 21 years, the same length of time that Joyce has been looking after the dining room. Karen, William and Martel, who help in this busy kitchen, have invested their loyalty too. Everything gets done, but there is no division into sections in this kitchen. Instead, long lists of jobs are put on the board every day and they are just seen to, almost invisibly. And there are hundreds of loyal customers. On a cold March day, when I had followed snow ploughs down a precarious M4 with forecasts telling everyone to stay at home, thirty people mysteriously appeared from nowhere for lunch – almost in loyalty to Franco.

Suppliers know Franco is a stickler for quality and it has taken him many years to persuade them to try growing different vegetables and fruits. And even when they conceded, Franco would be out with his tape measure rejecting beans that were too long or courgettes that were too thick. John Sullivan – now a well-known supplier in Abergavenny, who provides the crucial arterial supply to restaurants in the south west – was first encouraged by Franco. When Franco or Ann read about a new fruit or vegetable, John would do his best to get it. It's somehow incongruous in the middle of Abergavenny – with obsolete coal mines only seven miles away – to find every kind of produce from foie gras to quails' eggs to walnut oil to Parma ham. Certainly it's a far cry from the early sixties when Franco couldn't guarantee he'd get anything he ordered. But he still needs his small suppliers. Jock at the white house across the road supplies suckling pig for Franco's weekend dish of Porchetta; organic cheese is collected from Llanganog on their way back from the beach with Pavini; Graham and Glenys Watkins have even given up part of a field to grow roses for Franco's Rose Petal Ice Cream. And every Tuesday morning the W.I. stall is scrutinized – perhaps for mint or good parsley.

Two ingredients Franco supplies himself – truffles and wine. Back in Italy, Franco has ties with a truffle farm near Urbino, and large supplies of black and white truffles find their way to the Walnut Tree and from there to other restaurants in the south west. Franco at present pays around £250 per 1 kg/2¼ lb for truffles. Stored in Madeira they will keep for at least six months, which is why he can always use them so generously in his cooking. But although they may provide a garnish for many of his dishes, Franco believes they are best served simply with spaghetti and single cream – for it is dairy produce that best brings out the flavour of truffles.

The house wine at the Walnut Tree is a light Verdiccio which comes from the wine co-operative in Franco's home town of Montefano. Indeed the grapes from his own vineyards are in that wine: 'I can taste the soil of home when I drink it,' says Franco. However, Wales in many ways is more home for him than it is for Ann, for it is she who longs for Italy, not Franco. He can't bear to delegate, still less to leave the Walnut Tree, except for a week in November when he takes Pavini to Italy for half term.

For the rest of the year, the Walnut Tree is the centre of everything. 'There has to be a bit of Mama in every chef,' declares Franco, who has undoubtedly nurtured an extremely happy, family business in this whitewashed inn off the B4521. A walnut tree continues to flourish outside the door. Planted three weeks after they moved in, it is now, 25 years later, a sturdy, robust tree providing consistently delicious nuts – a testimony indeed to Franco and Ann Taruschio's Walnut Tree.

Zuppa di Vongole

Clam Soup

•

MAKES 2.25 L/4 PT

2.25 l/4 pt clams or small cockles
6 shallots, finely chopped
2 tbsp virgin olive oil
2 cloves of garlic, finely chopped
3 sprigs of parsley, chopped
a pinch of ground black pepper
150 ml/ ¼ pt dry white wine
wedges of lemon for garnish

•

1 Wash the clams and reject any that are open.
2 Sauté the shallots in the olive oil with the garlic, parsley and ground pepper for 2–3 minutes.
3 Add the clams and, when they have opened, pour in the wine.
4 Serve this soup with wedges of lemon.

In Wales, we use small cockles from Penclaudd.

'Thai' Fisherman's Soup

SERVES 8

900 g/2 lb Dublin Bay prawns
8 scallops
16 mussels
2 tbsp peanut oil
2.25 l/4 pt chicken stock
3 stalks of lemon grass, bruised
4 kaffir (or lime) leaves, bruised
1 tsp julienne of lime peel
1 green chilli, finely sliced
2 large limes
1 tbsp Nam Pia (Thai fish sauce)

•

GARNISH

•

kaffir, cut into thin julienne strips
red chilli, finely sliced
lemon grass, finely sliced

1 Peel the prawns and fry the shells in the peanut oil until they are pink.
2 Add the chicken stock, the lemon grass (cut into 1-cm/½-in lengths), kaffir leaves, lime peel and green chilli. Bring all this to the boil and simmer for 20 minutes.
3 Strain the mixture through a fine sieve and then bring to the boil again.
4 Cut the white meat of the scallops in half, leaving the coral attached to one half.
5 Add the prawns, mussels and scallops to the stock and cook for 2–3 minutes.
6 Lower the heat and add the juice of the limes and the Nam Pia.
7 Remove from the heat and serve decorated with the strips of kaffir, chilli and lemon grass.

Thai Mussels

SERVES 4 AS AN HORS D'OEUVRE

1.75 kg/4 lb mussels
8 cloves of garlic
1 large red chilli
2 tbsp peanut oil
2 tbsp Nam Pia (Thai fish sauce)
a small bunch of chopped mint

•

1 Scrub the mussels well and remove the beards (discard any that are cracked or open and do not shut immediately when tapped).
2 Chop the garlic and chilli finely – you could use a food mixer for this.
3 Heat the peanut oil in a frying pan and fry the garlic and chilli mixture until golden.
4 Add the Nam Pia followed by the mussels. Cover.
5 When the mussels have opened (this will take very little time), discard one half of the shell and place the mussels in the remaining shells on a serving dish (remove any mussels that have not opened).
6 Add the mint to the mussel juice, pour over the mussels and serve.

Oysters Gratinées with Laverbread

SERVES 4 AS AN HORS D'OEUVRE
24 oysters
100 g/3 ½ oz butter
1 small onion, finely chopped
1 dessertsp chopped parsley
juice of ½ lemon
salt and white pepper
200 g/7 oz laverbread
50 g/2 oz breadcrumbs

•

1 Open the oysters – reserving their juices – and place them in the deepest shell halves. Discard the shallow halves.
2 Mix together the butter, onion, parsley, lemon juice and half the oyster juice, and season with salt and pepper.
3 Spread the mixture over half the oysters, and cover the other half with laverbread.
4 Sprinkle with breadcrumbs and cook in the oven at 180°C/350°F/Gas Mark 4 for 4 minutes. Serve at once.

Anagosta con Salsa di Vin Santo

Lobster with a Sauce of Santo Wine

•

SERVES 4
4 lobsters, weighing 450 g/1 lb each
50 g/2 oz sultanas
175 ml/6 fl oz Vin Santo (sweet sherry can be substituted)
115 g/4 oz butter
a pinch of nutmeg, freshly grated
salt and freshly ground white pepper

•

1 Prepare the lobsters by removing the sand and sacs. They can be either boiled (3 minutes and then leave in the water for 5 minutes before draining) or grilled (they turn pink when cooked).
2 Place the sultanas in the Vin Santo to marinate.
3 Melt the butter in a pan and add a small pinch of nutmeg, a little salt and plenty of pepper.
4 When the butter is foaming, drain the Vin Santo and add to the pan. Cook until reduced by half, stirring from time to time.
5 Pour over the prepared lobster and sprinkle the sultanas over the dish.

Vin Santo is made from the white grapes which are hung on racks during winter then pressed during Easter Holy Week – hence its name.

Bresoala

half a topside of beef
best virgin olive oil
ground black pepper
wedges of lemon
chopped chives (optional)

•

MARINADE
enough red and white wine to cover the joint (equal amounts)
750 g/1 ¾ lb coarse sea salt
a large bunch of rosemary
12 bay leaves
24 cloves
3 cloves of garlic, crushed
40 black peppercorns
12 dry chillies
4 strips of orange peel

•

1 Trim the joint of beef, removing fat and sinews.
2 Put all the ingredients for the marinade in a large bowl, add the meat and leave for 1 week or until the meat feels firm.
3 Hang the meat in a dry, airy place for another week until it feels firm enough to be sliced thinly.
4 Rub the joint with olive oil, wrap in greaseproof paper and keep in the refrigerator until required.
5 To serve, slice it very thinly. Sprinkle with olive oil and season with pepper. Garnish with wedges of lemon and chopped chives if liked.

Bresoala PAGE 73

Franco Taruschio

Supreme of Pheasant, Cream, Carrots and Truffles PAGE 77

Brodetto

This dish is from the Marche region of Italy.

•

SERVES 6

1.6 kg/3 ½ lb fish (comprising fillets of red mullet, monkfish, whiting, gurnard and sole, mussels and Dublin Bay prawns, as available)
425 g/15 oz squid
1 onion, cut very finely
1 clove of garlic, crushed
olive oil
6 ripe tomatoes, chopped, peeled and de-seeded
150 ml/ ¼ pt dry white wine
white wine vinegar
425 g/15 oz plum tomatoes (tinned will do)
2 tbsp finely chopped parsley
chopped parsley for garnish
toast to serve

•

1 Clean the fish and cut into chunks. Clean the mussels and prawns – discard any mussels that are cracked or open and do not close when tapped.

2 Fry the onion and garlic in olive oil in a shallow casserole dish (preferably with two handles) until golden.

3 Clean the squid, slice finely, then add to the pan and cook for 3–4 minutes.

4 Add the chopped tomatoes, wine and a few drops of wine vinegar.

5 Sieve the plum tomatoes into the pan, add a little slightly salted water and cook until the squid is tender.

6 Add the chopped parsley, followed by the prawns and the thicker fish, then add the remaining fish.

7 Cover the pan and cook until the fish is just cooked. Remove from the heat and leave to settle (still keeping the lid on the pan).

8 Sprinkle parsley over the top of the fish and serve with toast.

Fegato con Cipolline Agro Dolce

Calves' Liver with Sweet and Sour Onions

•

SERVES 4

8 thin slices of calves' liver
flour (enough to coat the liver)
salt and pepper
virgin olive oil
150 ml/ ¼ pt sweet Marsala
70 ml/2 ½ fl oz dry sherry
70 ml/2 ½ fl oz brown stock
30 g/1 ¼ oz butter

•

SWEET AND SOUR ONIONS
750 g/1 ¾ lb baby onions
50 g/2 oz butter
30 g/1 ¼ oz sugar
70 ml/2 ½ fl oz wine vinegar
sage for garnish

•

1 Season the flour with salt and pepper and lightly coat the liver.

2 Heat a little oil in a frying pan and cook the liver for 3 minutes on each side.

3 Remove the liver from the pan and throw away any oil still remaining. Add the Marsala, sherry and brown stock, and cook until reduced by one-third.

4 Add the butter in knobs and stir off the heat until the sauce has thickened.

5 To make the sweet and sour onions, drop the onions in boiling water to make it easier to peel them.

6 Place the peeled onions in boiling water and boil for 5 minutes. Drain.

7 Melt the butter in a saucepan, add the sugar and stir over a medium heat for a few minutes.

8 Add the wine vinegar and continue to stir.

9 Add the onions and stir well. Cover the pan and place in the oven at 160°C/325°F/Gas Mark 3 for about 10 minutes or until golden.

10 Garnish with sage and serve with the liver.

Welsh Lamb with a Garlic Sauce

SERVES 6

6 best ends of Welsh lamb (each strip with 4 or 5 chops)
olive oil
2 eggs, beaten, for egg wash

•

HERB AND BREADCRUMB COATING

115 g/4 oz fresh breadcrumbs
1 tsp each chopped chervil, tarragon, thyme, parsley, chives and basil
salt and pepper

•

GARLIC SAUCE

3 heads of garlic (skins still intact)
300 ml/ ½ pt white wine
300 ml/ ½ pt water
300 ml/ ½ pt lamb stock
salt and pepper

•

GARNISH

30 cloves of garlic, peeled
olive oil
sprigs of thyme or mint

•

1 Trim the lamb, removing all the fat, and clean the bones up to the eye of the meat.
2 For the garnish, bring the peeled cloves of garlic to the boil in just enough water to cover them. Strain. Repeat this process with the garlic three times, then leave to cool.
3 Deep-fry the garlic cloves in olive oil until golden. Drain and leave on kitchen paper.
4 Make the sauce: leaving the skins on the garlic, gently bring the heads to the boil in the mixture of white wine, water and lamb stock. Cook until tender.
5 Pass the garlic mixture through a sieve, pressing well, then liquidize. Adjust the seasoning and consistency – you may need to add more water.
6 Seal the lamb in hot oil in a baking tray, then remove from the tray.
7 Mix breadcrumbs, herbs and seasoning.

8 Brush the outer surface of the lamb with the beaten egg and then cover with the breadcrumb mixture, pressing well to bind the crumbs.
9 Return the lamb to the baking tray and place in the oven at 190°C/375°F/Gas Mark 5 for about 7 minutes – or until the meat is pink. Remove from the oven and leave to rest for 4 minutes.
10 Carve the meat into chops.
11 Pour the garlic sauce onto the places and arrange the chops round each plate in a coronet shape. Garnish each serving with 5 garlic cloves and a sprig of thyme or mint.

Supreme of Pheasant, Cream, Carrots and Truffles

SERVES 4

4 breasts of hen pheasant
50 g/2 oz butter
50 ml/2 fl oz port
5 tbsp tomato-flavoured demi-glace (see below)
300 ml/ ½ pt double cream

•

GARNISH

20 g/ ¾ oz black truffle, cut into julienne strips
40 g/1 ½ oz carrots, cut into julienne strips and blanched

•

1 Fry the pheasant breasts, skin side down, in the butter until golden. Lower the heat and cook for 8 minutes, turn and cook for another 3 minutes.
2 Remove the breasts of pheasant and keep warm. Discard any excess butter and deglaze the pan with the port. Reduce it almost to nothing, then add the *demi-glace* and reduce again.
3 Add the double cream and reduce to thicken.
4 Pour the sauce onto the plates, place the pheasant breasts on top and garnish with the julienne strips of truffles and carrots.

A *demi-glace* is a stock based on veal, ham and game which has been cooked until reduced by half, and to which tomatoes have then been added.

Porchetta

Porchetta

In the area round Macerata on the east coast of central Italy, where this dish comes from, you can buy porchetta in every village. It is made for robust people – not figure watchers. And there is really no compromise – only a whole pig will yield true porchetta! Ask your butcher to bone the pig.

•

SERVES 12–14

1 small pig, weighing approx. 12 kg/25 lb
salt and pepper
a little oil
150 ml/ ¼ pt white wine
150 ml/ ¼ pt veal stock

•

STUFFING

a handful of rosemary
a handful of fennel leaves
1 head of garlic, peeled
liver and heart of pig, finely chopped
salt and ground black pepper

•

GARNISH

salad leaves
potatoes
rosemary
cloves of garlic

•

1 Season the inside of the pig, mix together the ingredients for the stuffing and use to stuff the pig.
2 Sew up the pig, place it on an oiled roasting tray and liberally season the outside.
3 Place in the oven at 240°C/475°F/Gas Mark 9 and cook for 3 hours, basting frequently.
4 When cooked, remove the pig and skim off the fat from the cooking juices.
5 Add the white wine and veal stock to the meat juices and cook until reduced by two-thirds.
6 Cut the porchetta into good slices and garnish with salad leaves. Serve with the sauce and accompany with roast potatoes cooked with fresh rosemary and garlic slivers.

Lasagne Bolognese

SERVES 4

•

PASTA

450 g/1 lb strong plain flour
3 eggs
175 g/6 oz cooked spinach, well drained and puréed
salt
2 dessertsp olive oil

•

RAGÙ BOLOGNESE

350 g/12 oz minced lean raw beef
85 g/3 oz bacon
olive oil
1 onion, finely chopped
1 carrot, finely chopped
2 sticks of celery, finely chopped
150 ml/ ¼ pt white wine
300 ml/ ½ pt water
3 tbsp tomato purée
2 sprigs of parsley, chopped
1 bay leaf
salt and pepper

•

BÉCHAMEL SAUCE

40 g/1 ½ oz butter
2 tbsp flour
750 ml/1 ¼ pt milk
salt and pepper
a pinch of nutmeg
85 g/3 oz Parmesan cheese, grated

•

1 To make the pasta, pour the flour into a mixing bowl and make a well in the centre. Lightly beat the eggs and then mix into the flour with the spinach and salt.

2 Work lightly into a rough ball and knead on a floured board for a few minutes until the dough is smooth, shiny and elastic. Wrap in greaseproof paper and leave for 30 minutes to rest.

3 If making by hand, divide the dough into four balls and flatten out each one, rolling lengthways. Keep the surface well floured. Continue until the pasta is paper-thin, then cut into wide strips.

4 Have ready a large pan of boiling water to which has been added a pinch of salt and the olive oil. Place the lasagne in the water and, when it rises to the top (this should take about 2 minutes), drain and dip straight away in a pan of cold water, then drain again. Leave on clean cloths.

5 To make the ragù, first mince the bacon and fry in a little olive oil.

6 Add the onion, carrot, celery and, when they have browned, add the beef and seal the meat.

7 Add the wine, water and tomato purée, parsley, bay leaf and seasoning, cover the pan and simmer for 30–40 minutes.

8 For the béchamel sauce, melt the butter in a saucepan, then add the flour and stir well.

9 Add the milk, which has been heated but not boiled, a little at a time, stirring all the time. Season with salt, pepper and nutmeg.

10 Cook for 15 minutes, stirring occasionally to ensure a creamy sauce.

11 Take a rectangular gratin dish (earthenware or stainless steel) approximately $30 \times 20 \times 7.5$ cm/ $12 \times 8 \times 3$ in; spread a layer of ragù bolognese in the bottom and then a layer of béchamel sauce. Sprinkle with Parmesan and cover with pasta.

12 Keep on layering in this way – ragù, then béchamel then Parmesan and then lasagne – until the dish is full, finishing with a layer of ragù bolognese, topped with béchamel sauce and a generous coating of Parmesan cheese.

13 Place the dish in the oven at 190°C/375°F/Gas Mark 5 for about 30 minutes. Serve bubbling hot.

Piedmontese Peppers

SERVES 4

2 red peppers
2 green peppers
8 fresh plum tomatoes, peeled (or other well-flavoured ripe tomatoes)
8 anchovy fillets
2 cloves of garlic, finely chopped
freshly ground pepper
virgin olive oil

1 Wash the peppers, cut in half and de-seed. Place them on a baking dish.

2 Place a plum tomato in each half of pepper and top with an anchovy fillet.

3 Scatter the garlic and freshly ground pepper over the peppers and sprinkle liberally with virgin olive oil.

4 Cover the dish with foil and cook in the oven at 190°C/375°F/Gas Mark 5 for about 20 minutes until *al dente*.

5 Serve hot or cold with plenty of Italian rough bread.

Radicchio Trevisano alla Griglia

Grilled Radicchio with Parmesan and Truffles

•

SERVES 8
4 heads of radicchio
3 tbsp virgin olive oil
salt and ground black pepper
115 g/4 oz Parmesan cheese, cut in fine slivers
2 white truffles, sliced into julienne strips

•

1 Remove any damaged leaves from the radicchio heads, cut each into four and wash thoroughly. Leave to drain in a colander.

2 Put the radicchio on a large plate and dribble the olive oil over the top. Season well with salt and ground black pepper.

3 Heat a large frying pan and, when hot, add the radicchio pieces in one layer only. Cover the pan, reduce the flame to moderate and cook for 2–3 minutes, turning the radicchio pieces once.

4 Arrange the Parmesan slivers on top of the radicchio and flash under a hot grill until the cheese has melted.

5 Top with the truffles and serve at once.

If a crispier version of this is desired, place the radicchio in a hot frying pan over a high heat and leave uncovered, turning once during the cooking time. Alternatively, the dish can be cooked on a grill over a charcoal fire.

Rose Petal Ice Cream

MAKES 600 ML/1 PT
8 egg yolks
175 g/6 oz caster sugar
450 ml/¾ pt milk
3 large red roses, highly perfumed (not sprayed with insecticides)
a few drops of rose water
crystallized rose petals for decoration

•

1 Mix the egg yolks and sugar together.

2 Bring the milk to the boil.

3 Add the milk to the egg and sugar mixture a little at a time, stirring constantly over a bain-marie. Remove from the heat and leave to cool.

4 Put the rose petals in the food processor with a little of the cooled custard and mix together.

5 Add the rose petal mixture to the rest of the custard with the rose water. Leave until cold.

6 Freeze in an ice cream maker (or see page 84). Serve decorated with crystallized rose petals.

Whimberry (or Bilberry) Sorbet

Bilberries are called whimberries in Wales and are very easy to find on the mountains around us.

•

SERVES 4–6
450 g/1 lb whimberries
115 g/4 oz sugar
150 ml/¼ pt water
juice of ½ lemon

•

1 Make a syrup by boiling the sugar and water together for 5 minutes. Allow to cool.

2 Sieve the raw whimberries and add the cooled syrup and lemon juice.

3 Pour the mixture into an ice cream making machine and work in the freezer for 5 minutes or until the paddles have stopped (or see page 84).

4 Serve with fresh cream and crystallized violets – or pour a little vodka over the sorbet – and decorate with fresh whimberries.

81

Robert Mey

Robert Mey remembers the puzzling sign at the back of his father's pastry shop in Besançon pointing to the '*laboratoire*'. Why should a pastry kitchen be referred to in such a scientific way when what was produced there was so artistic? Robert Mey Senior solemnly pointed out the crucially important sugar thermometer, the sacarometer (which measures the density of sugar in water) and the principles of fermentation as just three examples of the science of the pâtisserie. But Robert Mey Junior wasn't impressed – it was the delicate artistry in pastrywork which fascinated him.

Having been born above a pastry shop, in 1933, it was just as well that Robert Mey wanted to follow his father into the pastry kitchen – but even before he was old enough to start his apprenticeship he delighted in painting eggs for Easter or making '*bonne anniversaire*' plaques in sugar for birthday cakes. His first task as an apprentice, at the age of 16, was to butter the trays for the daily croissants – besides, of course, clearing up after everyone else. Progress came about three months later when he was allowed to help make *crème pâtissière*, separating egg yolks from the whites and weighing out the flour. However, he had to wait a few months more before he was allowed to mix the ingredients together. Combining work with a day-a-week college release, a traditional French apprenticeship takes three years; but Robert's father sent him halfway through it to a friend's pâtisserie to complete his training. There life was a lot easier for Robert – his father had been a hard task-master, and as the boss's son he had been forced to endure his colleagues' gibes if found guilty of bad time-keeping or a job less than well done.

Robert Mey's career was punctuated, as is that of every Frenchman, by two years of military service, after which he built up his experience in pastry shops in Reims, Bourbonne and Joinville. His move to England in 1957 was prompted not only by the desire to learn English, but also by his belief that working in a hotel would give him 'time to play with ingredients' – time to be more creative. Robert came to the Savoy in London, where in six years he moved through the ranks to *Chef Pâtissier* under Albon and the formidable Head Chef, Trumpetto. A large hotel like the Savoy is, of course, a world in itself, from day to day demanding a wide range of skills from its kitchen: and this is where Robert was able to 'play' with ingredients most ambitiously, creating chocolate confections, petit fours and centrepieces, and exercising his skills in sugarwork, pastillage, ice carving and cocoa painting. Using a canvas of marzipan and a French cocoa powder mixed with water, Robert literally paints pictures in cocoa, which gives a pleasing sepia effect to the image.

After the Savoy came a similar spell at the Coq d'Or – on the site now occupied by Langan's Brasserie. Then in 1969 Bernard Gaume, who had been a colleague at the Savoy, asked Robert to join him in heading the kitchens of the (now renamed) Hyatt Carlton Tower Hotel in Knightsbridge. The customary uneasiness between the Head Chef and his *Chef Pâtissier* was avoided by their longstanding respect for each other.

Just as at the Savoy, the pâtisserie has to produce whatever is required by the daily happenings in this busy hotel: plated desserts for the annual lunch of the Académie Culinaire; the daily sweet trolleys for the Chinoiserie tea room and the Rib Room; children's birthday parties complete with E.T. cakes; huge *croque-en-bouche* centrepieces or chocolate shoes filled with petits fours for the executive suites. Robert Mey will turn his hand to anything.

Robert no longer needs to enter competitions to prove his worth, but he has a photograph album crammed with pictures of his successes – such as the blue fighting lobsters made entirely from blown sugar for which he won a gold award. In his kitchen is an old plastic container containing mementoes of other competitions, including a piece of startlingly realistic French bread – made by pouring icing sugar into caramelized sugar, which bubbles through to produce the particularly airy texture. Another example is a piece of Brie which seems soft and creamy enough to eat. On top of a cupboard in the pâtisserie is an easel made of chocolate, complete with a marzipan canvas and oil paints made from sugar. Even the paint palate is edible – it's made from nougatine.

Now 54, Robert can look back over nearly forty years of pastry work and, although there have been flirtations with fashion, he believes the basic traditions remain. Crème caramel is still a favourite pudding and people will never tire of lemon meringue pie, Black Forest gâteau and Danish pastries. But Robert does acknowledge a movement away from the nouvelle cuisine displays of sorbets in pastry baskets back to rich crème brûlées and bread-and-butter pudding. And why not? Robert believes it is foolish to claim that it is possible to make truly light desserts: 'Most, let's face it, are rich; but what is wrong with serving just a small portion of a rich dessert?'

For preference, Robert selects cheese to end a meal, but his favourite dessert is a simple fruit salad – perhaps grapes, pineapple and orange mixed with a little lemon syrup to bring out their flavour, topped with some strawberries and then immersed in a good liqueur, and served with plain vanilla ice cream to bring out the true flavour of the fruit.

Robert hates to see the confusion of tastes that beset so many modern dishes. Of course taste buds blur when a savarin is soaked in a flavour syrup, topped with fruit that has been marinated in another set of flavours, decorated with cream that has been infused with another flavour, and served in a pool of sauce with its own different and distinctive taste. Robert is convinced that it is quite enough to soak a savarin in rum syrup and then add just one more taste – say, apricots – to produce a strong, clearly defined and delicious pudding.

Since 1970, Robert Mey has been the Chief Examiner for the City and Guilds' Institute Advanced Pastry course, and it is here that he meets students about to begin their careers in pastrywork. Robert's simple message to them is to concentrate on the flavour of everything they prepare. Faced with two cakes, and one looking better than the other, Robert makes flavour the final arbiter. Presentation is important, but he believes it has been given undue emphasis: it's not enough just to titillate a complicated plate. Robert has seen too many students trying to run before they can even crawl, but their situation is far from perfect: catering courses are too short; students' expectations are too high; wages are low; and the system of reward is too rigid. When Robert was an apprentice, if real progress was made a young person would be given a bonus: now everyone is rewarded in the same way in a system which takes no account of merit. It's a familiar argument in the hotel industry that low wages don't attract the right people but do create ideal conditions for the 'cowboys' of the industry who have no respect for traditional skills. This makes it difficult to preserve high standards of service in the kitchen and dining room – standards which are second nature to people like Robert Mey.

Crème Anglaise

Custard Cream

•

MAKES 1L/1¾PT
12 egg yolks
225 g/8 oz caster sugar
1 l/1 ¾ pt milk
1 vanilla pod

•

1 Whisk the yolks and sugar, so that the mixture forms soft peaks and the whisk leaves a trail.
2 Put the milk and vanilla in a pan and bring to the boil; pour this over the whisked mixture.
3 Return the mixture to the saucepan and cook for a few minutes, stirring continuously with a wooden spoon in a figure-of-eight motion, until the mixture thickens and coats the spoon. Do not overcook as the mixture may curdle; should this occur, add a few drops of water or spirit and whisk to return the mixture to a smooth texture.
4 Pass the mixture through a fine sieve and cool immediately on crushed ice to prevent the formation of bacteria.

Crème Anglaise is used as a basis for dessert sauces and ice cream, and is an ingredient of other desserts such as bavarois and charlotte mousses.

Glace à la Vanille

Vanilla Dairy Ice Cream

Make the Crème Anglaise (see above), and when the mixture is cool, freeze in an ice cream maker.

If you have not got an ice cream maker, put the mixture in a shallow freezing container and freeze until the ice cream is half frozen. Turn the mixture out into a cold bowl, break down with a fork or whisk, then beat until smooth. Return to the container and freeze until completely firm.

To obtain a particularly rich, smooth and light ice cream, substitute double cream for 30 per cent of the milk content in the original recipe.

Honey Ice Cream

Make the Crème Anglaise, substituting 115 g/4 oz of honey for an equal weight of the sugar in the original recipe. Cool and freeze as for Glace à la Vanille. Serve with a spoonful of honey on top.

Praline Ice Cream

Make the Crème Anglaise, substituting 115 g/4 oz of praline for an equal weight of sugar in the original recipe, and add 50 ml/2 fl oz of rum. Cool and freeze as for Glace à la Vanille.

Bavarois à la Vanille

Vanilla Bavarois

•

SERVES 8
3 eggs
50 g/2 oz caster sugar
250 ml/9 fl oz milk
¼ vanilla pod
10 g/ ¼ oz gelatine powder
250 ml/9 fl oz double cream

•

1 Whisk the eggs and sugar to a light texture, as for Crème Anglaise (see above). Bring the milk and vanilla to the boil and pour on to the mixture.
2 Add the gelatine powder while the mixture is still warm. Strain, and cool to near setting point. Whip the double cream and add it to the mixture.
3 Fill a 1-litre/1¾-pt bavarois fluted mould. Allow the dessert to chill for 2 hours before removing it from the mould, and serve.

Chocolate Bavarois

Follow step 1 (above) and add 50 g/2 oz of melted chocolate and a tablespoon of dark rum to the warm *crème* before mixing. Proceed as for Bavarois à la Vanille.

Chestnut Bavarois

Follow step 1 above and add 50 g/2 oz of chestnut purée to the *crème* while it is still warm. Proceed as for Bavarois à la Vanille.

All bavarois can be served with Crème Anglaise (see page 84) as a sauce, flavoured with a liqueur of your choice, or with whipped cream.

Oeufs à la Neige

Snow Eggs

•

SERVES 8

8 egg whites (at room temperature)
a pinch of salt
225 g/8 oz caster sugar
600 ml/1 pt Crème Anglaise (see page 84)
1 ½ tbsp Kirsch
50 g/2 oz toasted flaked almonds
icing sugar for decoration

•

1 Beat the egg whites and salt to a stiff snow using a whisk or a mixer. Fold in the caster sugar very carefully using a wooden spoon.
2 Bring 600 ml/1 pt of water to the boil in a shallow saucepan. Using two large spoons, scoop out some meringue, the size of an egg, and place in the boiling water. Allow to poach for 3 minutes each side. Repeat until the meringue mixture is completely used up.
3 Drain the snow eggs by lifting them out in a slotted spoon, and place them on an absorbent cloth.
4 Flavour the Crème Anglaise with the Kirsch. Fill the bottom of a deep china or glass dish with this sauce.
5 Place the snow eggs on top and cover with the remainder of the sauce. Sprinkle with toasted flaked almonds and dust with icing sugar.

Crème Brûlée

SERVES 6

600 ml/1 pt double cream
1 egg
5 egg yolks
115 g/4 oz caster sugar
3 drops vanilla essence
3 tbsp rum or brandy
115 g/4 oz brown sugar

•

1 Boil the cream, then combine the egg, egg yolks, sugar, vanilla and rum or brandy, and fill six ramekins or one large dish.
2 Cook in a bain-marie at 160°C/325°F/Gas Mark 3 until set – about 40–55 minutes.
3 Sprinkle the surface with brown sugar and grill under full heat until golden brown in colour.

Fruit also goes well under the *crème*.

Nougat Glacé

SERVES 8

115 g/4 oz good quality honey
3 egg whites
50 g/2 oz glacé cherries, finely chopped
50 g/2 oz whole pistachio nuts, shelled
50 g/2 oz orange peel, finely chopped
1 soupsp Kirsch (or eau-de-vie)
600 ml/1 pt double cream
50 g/2 oz nibbed almonds, roasted
50 g/2 oz flaked almonds, roasted

•

1 Place the honey in a saucepan and heat to 125°C/250°F.
2 Beat the egg whites until stiff and pour the honey over the top. Beat until cold.
3 Add cherries, nuts, peel and Kirsch.
4 Lightly whip the cream and fold it into the mixture. Add the nibbed and flaked almonds.
5 Pour into a small loaf tin (450-g/1-lb size). Freeze and serve in slices when required. Dip tin in warm water for a few seconds to unmould.

Crème Brûlée PAGE 85

Robert Mey

Millefeuille Napoléon PAGE 88

Millefeuille Napoléon

SERVES 6

•

PUFF PASTRY
115 g/4 oz strong plain flour
a pinch of salt
115 g/4 oz butter
50 ml/2 fl oz ice-cold water

•

PASTRY CREAM
3 egg yolks
50 g/2 oz caster sugar
25 g/1 oz flour
300 ml/ ½ pt milk
vanilla pod
1 tsp Kirsch

•

CRÈME FOUETTÉE
300 ml/1 pt double cream
50 g/2 oz icing sugar or *caster sugar*
a few drops of vanilla essence

•

FOR SERVING
icing sugar for sprinkling
450 g/1 lb fresh strawberries
150 ml/ ¼ pt strawberry coulis

•

1 Prepare the pastry: make a dough with the flour, salt, 15 g/ ½ oz of the butter and the water. Mix well.

2 Mould the dough into a ball and, using a sharp knife, score across the top to relax the dough. Cover with a cloth and leave to rest in the refrigerator for ½ –1 hour.

3 Roll the dough into a square, with the corners rolled more thinly than the centre.

4 Place the remainder of the butter in the centre of the dough square and close the four corners to form an envelope.

5 Roll out the envelope into a rectangle 25 × 15 cm/10 × 6 in, and fold in three. This forms a normal 'turn'.

6 Repeat the same operation immediately – you have now given two 'turns'.

7 Rest the dough for 1 hour in the refrigerator.

8 Repeat stages 5 and 6 – you have now given four 'turns'. Rest the dough again for 1 hour.

9 Repeat stages 5 and 6 – you have now given six 'turns'. Rest the dough for 1 hour, and the puff pastry is ready to use.

10 Roll the puff pastry into a thin rectangular sheet and place on a greased baking tray. Allow the pastry to rest in a cold place for 1 hour.

11 Bake in the oven at 220°C/425°F/Gas Mark 7 for 15 minutes. Turn over and bake for a further 10 minutes.

12 Sprinkle with sugar and cool before using.

13 Prepare the pastry cream: whisk the egg yolks and sugar to a fluffy texture. Add the flour and mix well.

14 Boil the milk and vanilla pod. Remove the pod – it can be used again in other recipes. Pour half the milk over the mixture and stir well. Then pour the mixture into the remainder of the milk.

15 Bring to the boil, whisking continuously for a few minutes. Remove from the heat immediately and pour into a basin. Cover with buttered greaseproof paper and allow to cool before using.

16 Prepare the *crème fouettée* by whipping together all the ingredients.

17 Prepare the millefeuille: cut the pastry sheet into three equal pieces. Top the first layer with pastry cream mixed with the Kirsch. Place on top a second layer of pastry, followed by pastry cream, cover with *crème fouettée* and strawberries, points to the top. Place a third layer of pastry on top of the strawberries, and cover the top and sides with a thin layer of *crème fouettée*.

18 Sprinkle the top with icing sugar, burn with a hot iron bar or poker, decorate with halved strawberries and serve with strawberry coulis (fresh strawberries liquidized with a sugar syrup and, if desired, some liqueur).

Pomponettes au Rhum

These are similar to Rum Babas.

•

MAKES 12 INDIVIDUAL POMPONETTES

•

SAVARIN PASTE
25 ml/1 fl oz warm milk
10 g/ ¼ oz yeast
115 g/4 oz plain strong flour
2 eggs
10 g/ ¼ oz sugar
a pinch of salt
50 g/2 oz melted butter

•

SOAKING SYRUP
225 g/8 oz water
115 g/4 oz sugar
25 ml/1 fl oz rum

•

FOR SERVING
115 g/4 oz apricot purée
300 ml/ ½ pt Crème Fouettée
(see Millefeuille recipe on page 88)

•

1 Prepare the savarin dough: mix the warm milk with the yeast and 25 g/1 oz of flour to produce a ferment. Leave for a few minutes, then add the remainder of the flour, the eggs, sugar and salt. Mix to an elastic dough.

2 Put the melted butter on top and prove in a warm place (30°C/86°F) until the dough has doubled in volume.

3 Beat the dough until the butter is well incorporated. Then half-fill twelve 5-cm/2-in diameter greased and floured tartlet moulds, and leave to prove in a warm place until doubled in volume.

4 Bake in the oven at 220°C/425°F/Gas Mark 7 for 15–20 minutes.

5 Prepare the soaking syrup: slowly heat the water, sugar and rum in a saucepan to allow the sugar to dissolve.

6 Using a small 'spider' (slotted) spoon, dip each *pomponette* into the hot syrup until soft and soaked with the rum syrup.

7 Remove from the syrup and place on a cooling rack, allowing the syrup to drain. Brush the tops with hot apricot purée.

8 When cold, slice in half with a sharp knife, and fill with *crème fouettée*.

Pomponettes can be plated and served with apricot coulis (fresh apricots liquidized with a sugar syrup and, if desired, some liqueur). If required, more rum can be added before serving.

Banana Nelusko

SERVES 6
6 bananas
300 ml/ ½ pt pastry cream
(see Millefeuille recipe on page 88)
115 g/4 oz melted chocolate
70 ml/2 ½ fl oz dark rum
600 ml/1 pt whipped cream
(see Millefeuille recipe)
50 g/2 oz grated chocolate
25 g/1 oz icing sugar

•

1 Prepare the filling: mix together the pastry cream, melted chocolate and rum, and fold in the whipped cream.

2 Lay one banana flat. Remove the top third of the skin to create a 'canoe', and gently remove the fruit. Treat all the bananas in this way.

3 Half-fill each banana-skin canoe with some of the filling.

4 Slice the bananas lengthways and replace in the canoes, arranged on top of the filling.

5 Cover the bananas with more of the filling. Top with grated chocolate and sprinkle with icing sugar.

Lime Chiffon Pie PAGE 92

Brioche Pudding PAGE 94

Lime Chiffon Pie

SERVES 6

•

SWEET PASTRY CASE
115 g/4 oz unsalted butter
50 g/2 oz sugar
1 egg
225 g/8 oz plain flour

•

FILLING
2 limes
2 leaves gelatine
2 eggs, separated
115 g/4 oz caster sugar
zest of 1 lemon
a few drops of green food colouring (optional)

•

DECORATION
spun sugar decoration
1 lime
mint leaves

•

1 Prepare the pastry case: cream the butter and sugar, add the egg and mix to a smooth texture. Fold in the flour.
2 Roll out the dough, and line a 20-cm/8-in flan tin with it.
3 Bake 'blind' in the oven at 200°C/400°F/Gas Mark 6 until cooked – about 15 minutes.
4 To make the filling: soak the gelatine leaves in cold water until softened.
5 Grate the zest and squeeze the juice of the limes.
6 Whisk the egg yolks with 50 g/2 oz of the caster sugar until light and fluffy, and add the zest of lime and lemon.
7 Drain the water from the soaked gelatine. In a separate container, add the gelatine to the lime juice; warm slightly over a saucepan of hot water to melt the gelatine.
8 Whisk the egg whites to a stiff meringue and add the remaining caster sugar.
9 Slowly pour the melted gelatine and lime juice into the meringue, then fold this mixture into the yolks, lime and lemon zest and caster sugar. Scoop the mixture into the baked pastry case. A few drops of green food colouring may be added to the final mixture if desired.
10 Allow the mixture to set in the refrigerator (about 1 hour).
11 If you are using the double cream, whip it and stir in the icing sugar.
12 Slice the lime pie into six equal portions, and decorate each portion as you like with a thin twisted slice of lime and/or a mint leaf. Place the sugar decoration in the middle.

Escoffier Baskets

MAKES 10–12 BASKETS
115 g/4 oz caster sugar
50 g/2 oz butter
115 g/4 oz golden syrup
50 g/2 oz plain flour
115 g/4 oz melted plain chocolate

•

1 Make a brandy-snap paste: cream together the sugar and butter, and add the golden syrup. Finally add the sieved flour and mix the ingredients well together. Keep in the refrigerator until ready to use. (As well as the Escoffier baskets, the paste can be used to make rolled Cigarette Brandy Snaps which are filled with whipped cream.)
2 To make one basket, take 25 g/1 oz of paste and shape it into a smooth ball.
3 Make balls of paste until it is all used, and place them on a greased baking tray. Cook in the oven at 220°C/425°F/Gas Mark 7 until the mixture has spread and is golden in colour. This will take about 8–10 minutes.
4 Leave to cool, until it is possible to mould each piece into a basket shape. Use a small glass dish to help form the basket.
5 When cold, brush the outside with melted chocolate. The baskets can be used for serving peaches, pears, strawberries, sorbets etc., and keep well in a freezer.

Les Poires Dijonnaises

Poached Pears in a Cassis Sauce

•

SERVES 4

4 large fresh pears (Comice or William pears are best)
25 g/1 oz cornflour
120 ml/4 fl oz cassis liqueur (blackcurrant)
115 g/4 oz fresh or tinned blackcurrants

•

SYRUP
1.2 l/2 pt water
225 g/8 oz caster sugar
1 cinnamon stick

•

DECORATION
4 mint leaves
2 cinnamon sticks

•

1 Prepare the syrup: put the water, sugar and cinnamon into a saucepan and bring to the boil.
2 Peel the fresh pears, and poach in the syrup until tender. Do not boil.
3 Prepare the cassis sauce: using half of the poaching syrup, mix a little with the cornflour, then add the rest of the syrup and the cassis liqueur and warm gently, stirring until thickened.
4 Cover the bases of the individual dishes, or of one large serving dish, with some sauce and the blackcurrants.
5 Place the poached pears in the dishes, cover each pear with the remainder of the sauce, and decorate each with a mint leaf and half a cinnamon stick.

This sweet is ideal served with a lemon sorbet and cookies.

Moist Fruit Cake

FOR A 15-CM/6-IN CAKE
50 g/2 oz sultanas
50 g/2 oz currants
50 g/2 oz mixed peel
50 g/2 oz glacé cherries
50 ml/2 fl oz brandy or dark rum
115 g/4 oz unsalted butter
50 g/2 oz caster sugar
50 g/2 oz brown sugar
2 eggs
115 g/4 oz plain flour
10 g/¼ oz baking powder

•

1 Soak the fruit in brandy or rum for a minimum of 24 hours before use.
2 Gently cream the unsalted butter, caster sugar and brown sugar. For the best results, the ingredients used for the preparation of the mix should be at room temperature.
3 Add the eggs, one at a time. Add the flour, sieved, and the baking powder.
4 Add the soaked fruit, mixed peel and cherries. Mix well.
5 Pour the mixture into a 15-cm/6-in cake tin lined with aluminium foil.
6 Bake in the oven at 180°C/350°F/Gas Mark 4 for 1½ hours. Place a pan of water in the oven to maintain a humid atmosphere – this ensures thorough cooking and results in a flat-topped cake.
7 When cold, wrap the fruit cake in foil to retain the moisture. Always use a very sharp knife to cut the cake to prevent crumbling.

Brioche Paste

MAKES 1 LOAF OR 8 INDIVIDUAL BRIOCHES
225 g/8 oz strong plain flour
50 ml/2 fl oz warm milk
15 g/ ½ oz baker's yeast
25 g/1 oz caster sugar
a pinch of salt
2 eggs
115 g/4 oz butter
1 egg, beaten, for egg wash
•

1 Prepare the basic dough: mix the warm milk and yeast with a little flour in a mixing bowl – this forms the ferment. Leave for a few minutes to become frothy.
2 Add the remainder of the flour, sugar, salt and eggs, and beat until smooth. Add the butter, and mix until the mixture starts to be elastic.
3 Cover the paste with clingfilm and prove in a warm place (24°C/75°F) until the dough has doubled in size (about 1 hour).
4 Push down the paste, cover again with clingfilm, and place in the refrigerator. Leave for a few hours before using.
5 To make a brioche loaf, lightly grease a 450-g/ 1-lb loaf tin. Smooth the paste by rolling it into an oblong shape, and place it in the greased loaf tin. Prove in a warm place (24°C/75°F) until double in volume. Then brush carefully with egg wash, using a very soft brush, and bake in the oven at 220°C/425°F/Gas Mark 7 for about 35 minutes.
6 To make individual brioches, divide the paste into eight equal portions and shape them into balls. Place in brioche moulds and prove in a warm place (24°C/75°F). When doubled in volume, carefully brush with egg wash, using a very soft brush. Bake in the oven at 220°C/425°F/Gas Mark 7 for 20 minutes.

Brioche Lorraine

Make the brioche paste as above and roll it out to a large oval. Fill the centre with pastry cream (see Millefeuille recipe on page 88) and sultanas which have been soaked in Kirsch.

Fold up the paste as an envelope and turn it upside down on a buttered baking tray. Prove in a warm place (24°C/75°F) until doubled in volume. Before baking, carefully brush with egg wash, using a very soft brush. Bake in the oven at 220°C/425°F/Gas Mark 7 for 35 minutes.

Brioche Pudding

The originality of this dish is the fact you do not have to soak the brioche with melted butter because of the high butter content already in the brioche.
•

SERVES 4
3 thin slices of brioche (see Brioche Paste above)
25 g/1 oz sultanas, soaked in Kirsch
150 ml/ ¼ pt double cream
150 ml/ ¼ pt milk
50 g/2 oz sugar
½ vanilla pod
2 eggs, beaten
•

1 Cut the brioche slices into triangles, and cover the bottom of a 600-ml/1-pt pie dish. Sprinkle with the sultanas.
2 Bring the double cream, milk, sugar and vanilla pod to the boil. Mix with the beaten egg.
3 Pass the mixture through a sieve, and pour it over the brioche and sultanas.
4 Bake over hot water in a bain-marie in the oven at 190°C/375°F/Gas Mark 5 until the custard is set – between 35 and 40 minutes.
5 Glaze under a hot grill before serving.

Index

Index